YOUNG AND DISAFFECTED

YOUNG AND DISAFFECTED

SOME (BITTERSWEET) NOTES FOR GROWING UP SOUTHERN

VALENCIA RICHARDSON

NEW DEGREE PRESS

YOUNG AND DISAFFECTED

Some (bittersweet) notes for growing up Southern

ISBN   978-1-64137-365-4   *Paperback*

978-1-64137-710-2   *Ebook*

To my nieces and nephews and all others still growing up,
may we create a better world in which you feel at home.

CONTENTS

INTRODUCTION

———

We take two steps forward
They take one step backward
We take each step to lift us up Higher

- SERATONES, "POWER"

"We passed the bill!" I exclaimed into the phone.

I was wound tight.

When I picked up the phone and called my mentor, Nadia, to tell her the good news I screamed it to her before she even got the chance to say hello.

∗ ∗ ∗

With the cacophony of cheers in the background, I drifted away from the moment and onto more existential thoughts.

Barely twenty-one years old, I was a recent college graduate and now a makeshift lobbyist. In spite of the achievement, the moment felt slightly less victorious and slightly more anti-climactic. Myself and my classmates mostly planned as we went, and everything had gone our way—for the most part, our legislative action proved successful. Barely in our twenties, we had passed a law that we came up with. We worked hard, drafting our proposal, and working with classmates at the Manship School of Mass Communication. I remember testifying for our bill in front of the Louisiana legislature and feeling patronized by the elected officials on the committee; as we spoke about the work we did at Louisiana State University assisting students in voting and registering to vote, the legislators all but patted us on the back for all the hard work we had done.

They looked at us like cute kids. Still, the bill passed the committee and eventually both chambers of the state legislature, so I could not think about that too much.

As the last year flashed through my memory, my thoughts quickly turned toward the future. I knew that in a few short months, I would be headed off to Mexico City to embark on a Fulbright scholarship and eventually to law school somewhere else, away from Louisiana for the first time in my life.

But that day was different. First, I could not stop sweating.

The Baton Rouge sun beat down on the long, narrow concrete corridor that connects the Louisiana Capitol building to downtown. I should not have been surprised—it was June of 2016, and a hot day in Louisiana is as expected as sunrise and sunset. Still, I couldn't help but notice the heat waves.

The nerves exacerbated the sweating.

Nadia screamed in my ear, putting me on speaker phone and telling the rest of the team at The Andrew Goodman Foundation that Louisiana House Bill 940 had officially become law and public universities across the state would have to make their student IDs voter ID compliant—a victory for thousands of students. I notified the rest of the team, including my other mentors, Bob Mann and Len Apcar. While I was still on the phone with Nadia, I remembered the voices on the phone fading into the background.

The sweaty, passion-and-nerve-filled woman that day felt alive.

Nerves faded into calm.

Calm made way for more thoughts about what this all meant.

* * *

What did I care?

After all, I had spent the better part of my short life vowing to get away from this place that had caused me so much trouble—I never felt like I belonged in my hometown of Shreveport, Louisiana, or anywhere in the South for that matter. Sure, I felt "Southern," and I liked all the cool things that people from the South enjoyed—our music, our food, our kindness toward strangers. Still, this place was toxic to me. Like I would never be given a good faith shot.

For a long time, Shreveport and Louisiana and the South represented to me everything that I was supposed to run away from. I was supposed to get good grades, work hard, and make it out to more successful prospects. I was always just a Black girl from the boondocks and I needed to get away to somewhere that wasn't so racist, so backwards, so UGH.

As it turned out, I did care.

I slowly came to the understanding that maybe I didn't need Louisiana, but Louisiana needed me. More specifically, Louisiana needed people who were willing to stay and do the work. We just won huge in the state legislature—managing to get unanimous, bipartisan support on a bill that affected more than 100,000 college students in the state. We convinced people of a greater good, and of a common sense solution to an unnecessary, arbitrary barrier. We needed to do more—community colleges and private universities were left out of the bill, and there was much to be done in other areas of youth voting rights in the state.

I could have stayed full-time and play a more direct role in growing the organization that we built, and train the students that came after me. I could have gone to law school in Louisiana instead of choosing Georgetown University Law Center more than one thousand miles away from Baton Rouge. I needed to stay, but I left. While I am still a resident of Louisiana, still do work there, and plan to come back permanently, I feel a constant guilt for deciding not to stay on the ground full-time.

My story is not unfamiliar. Like many young people in the South, I reached the crossroads between staying and going; between fighting the good fight and giving myself a break. I am constantly in awe of the young folks who decided to keep pushing that rock up the mountain with conviction and without regret.

After all, the most consequential moment in the history of the Deep South and the United States—the Civil Rights

Movement—would not have been as successful without the sacrifice of young people. John Lewis got his start in the Student Nonviolent Coordinating Committee. Martin Luther King, Jr. became president of the Southern Christian Leadership Conference when he was just twenty-eight—and began working on the campaign for the South during his time at Morehouse College. James Chaney, Michael Schwerner, and Andrew Goodman were twenty-one, twenty-four, and twenty when they were killed during Mississippi Freedom Summer in 1964 for the crime of trying to register Black residents to vote; a few months later, the Civil Rights Act of 1964 was passed and the Voting Rights Act passed a year later.

The fight for progress in the South rages on today, but the determination of young people rages alongside. On Valentine's Day in 2018, a gunman took the lives of seventeen students and faculty members at Marjorie Stoneman Douglas High. The region, and the world, was taken by storm by a group of high school students who decided that they wanted to be the last victims of a school shooting in America. The activism of March for Our Lives has led for gun law reform across the country, but their effect has reverberated to young people across the South who are now seeking ways to make changes of their own.

In the 2018 midterm elections, we saw the rise of two candidates thought to be impossible. Andrew Gillum (Florida) and Stacey Abrams (Georgia) ran for statewide office and gave the rest of the nation reason to look South again for electoral victory. Lost in their narrow defeats, however, is the long history of dedicating their lives to their states which sets the backdrop for their influential careers.

Both Gillum and Abrams actively refused to give up on their homes as young college students in Florida and Georgia, respectively. Their trajectory was not in fact unexpected, but rather the cultivation of a movement that they themselves began as young college students. Andrew Gillum became the youngest city commissioner in Tallahassee, Florida at a mere twenty-three years old, and Stacey Abrams took to protesting as a student at Spelman College, burning the old Georgia state flag in protest of the Confederacy.

And finally, when the Unite the Right Rally raged the small college town of Charlottesville, Virginia, killing one person and injuring others, the Black Students Union at the University of Virginia led the charge in demanding substantive change to the university's storied history of racism and its outdated diversity and inclusion policies. While their trauma persists, the Black student leaders of the University of Virginia nevertheless have gifted the region with a masterclass in demanding reconciliation after trauma that will outlast their time as students.

The promise of progress in the South began with young people, and its promises will be fulfilled by young people.

The young people who decide to stay and do the on-the-ground work of progressing the South have always had lessons to teach. We rely on the human capital that is the young organizer to make small movements in the South, but forget to look at their capacity to create broad change. For several months, I researched organizers, activists, and leaders, and also talked to a few of them, across the Deep South to learn why they decided to stay and do their work at home. Their connection to me is not a coincidence; the network of young Southern organizers is strong, and we are looking for other young folks to join us. The motivations, goals, successes, and contradictions of the identities in this book reveal that though we may have a lot to learn, we as young people also have a lot to teach.

The South is not a monolith, nor are its people. The story of the young Southerner refusing to cede ground to injustice, however, is a story that transcends time. The story of the young Southerner is but living memory that threads from the very origins of the freedom movement in the region. Put simply, younger generations have been doing this for a long time—we just need to figure out how to support them more. What I learned from them, and from my own experiences, paints a portrait of a hopeful future for the region.

It feels bittersweet, but we are not giving up on the place that raised us.

CHAPTER 1

GETTING STARTED

———

Tell about the South. What's it like there. What do they do there.
Why do they live there. Why do they live at all.

- WILLIAM FAULKNER, ABSALOM! ABSALOM!

The South.

In this day and age, there is no clearly defined boundary.

Perhaps most people understand broadly that the "South" signifies the Southeastern region of the United States. I'd also venture that the "Deep South" usually refers to the states along the Gulf Coast—Louisiana, Mississippi, Alabama, and Florida.

GETTING STARTED · 17

When I get into debates with people on this topic, the question tends to gravitate toward whether the "South" is defined by Civil War lines; in other words, which states were a part of the Confederacy. Others quip that the line between North and South is marked by the Mason-Dixon line, which would place every state below Pennsylvania in the mix. If the Confederacy was the universal definition, then defining the physical boundaries is simple—the former Confederacy consisted of Alabama, Arkansas, Florida, Georgia, Louisiana, Mississippi, North Carolina, South Carolina, Tennessee, Texas, and Virginia.[1] There is considerable debate regarding which of these states actually comprise the South, though I'd bet almost no one would deny that these states constitute the "South" by definition.

There are still so many questions that accompany this broad definition, however.

Does South Florida, which includes Miami, constitute the South?

Northern Virginia, near Washington, D.C.?

Washington, D.C. itself?

---

1   "Confederate States of America," Britannica, last updated August 13, 2019, https://www.britannica.com/topic/Confederate-States-of-America.

Texas?

Oklahoma?

Southern Missouri?

Is Kentucky considered Appalachian or Southern, or both?

What about coal country in Northern Alabama?

Will North Carolina, with its staunchly purple politics, soon no longer be considered "Southern"?

Is the Confederacy still an accurate marker of the South, when one can find a Confederate flag in the obviously-not-Southern region of upstate New York or the state of Oregon?

When will the Confederate definition no longer be appropriate, as more Southerners have begun to reject its ideals and call for confrontation of the violent, evil past that the Confederacy represents?

Why is the Confederate flag an appropriate marker anyway, given its symbolism to white supremacy and the fact that the region comprises the largest population of Black people in America?

What is "Southern," anyway?

Frankly, does geography truly even matter in today's digital and transient world?

More importantly, who gets to define being "Southern"?

There may wind up being more questions here than answers. And that's part of the drive behind this book.

* * *

There is considerable data that forms the conclusion that no one knows what *really* constitutes the South, at least not in the universal sense. One poll by *Five Thirty Eight* found that some survey respondents considered the South to stretch as far west as Arizona and Colorado, and as far north as Delaware and Pennsylvania.[2] Another story by *AL.com*, which ultimately decided that South "depends on who you're talking to," note a number of markers which can change the composition of the region, including the "Bible Belt," "Dixie," and even the availability of sweet tea.[3]

---

2   Walt Hickey, "Which States Are in the South?" Five Thirty Eight, April 30, 2014, https://fivethirtyeight.com/features/which-states-are-in-the-south/.

3   AL.com, "What is the South?," published August 2, 2017, https://www.youtube.com/watch?v=7SGYkajXtb8.

The 2010 U.S. Census found that the majority of the country's Black population lived in the South—which it defined as Alabama, Arkansas, Delaware, the District of Columbia, Florida, Georgia, Kentucky, Louisiana, Maryland, Mississippi, North Carolina, Oklahoma, South Carolina, Tennessee, Texas, Virginia, and West Virginia.[4] Defining the South becomes much more difficult when factoring in the social, political, and cultural landscape—vast and varied, Southern culture is not so easily bound by physical borders.

In this book, I intentionally decline to adopt a hard-line definition of the South because I believe that being Southern is mostly about self-identification.

Many people throw around the idea of a "New South," an idea which generally refers to the economic transformation of liberal Southern cities, including well-known places like Atlanta, Georgia; Nashville, Tennessee; or Austin, Texas. Undoubtedly, a theme throughout this book is that a foundational aspect of being Southern is reckoning with Southern history, which cannot ignore the Confederacy. This does not mean, however, that those who benefited from the Confederacy get to continue to define what it means to be Southern. Rather, an integral part of defining the term should include how the most marginalized self-identify with the region. In other

---

4   "The Black Population: 2010," U.S. Census Bureau, September 2011, https://www.census.gov/prod/cen2010/briefs/c2010br-06.pdf.

words, what does it mean to be Southern and Black or brown, Southern and gay, Southern and non-Christian?

Self-identification, then, is the primary method by which one should define being Southern.

While I did consider the general principles of the Confederate South as a general starting point, the people, places, and events that I researched, spoke to, witnessed, and studied are self-identified Southerners. Their personal backgrounds vary, but they had the common connection of their steadfast dedication to their home states or the region at large.

The basis of self-identification as a Southern likewise varies. One can associate the culture with Southern hospitality or Southern religion; Southern conservative politics Southern progressive movements; Southern music and literature or Southern history. Self-identification can include being born in the South, or being raised there; maybe one is simply a transplant who decided to make the South home.

Whatever the case, being Southern cannot be defined by the region's predominantly-told history. Indeed, to capture an entire region based on the evil of the antebellum reduces the history of those whose humanity was denied; those lost in this imposed definition are those most marginalized, not those who commit and benefit from the atrocity.

Self-identification as a Southerner is all the more important in recognizing that the region is also the home to people of color, to non-Christians, to queer people, and to differently-abled people; the South is more than the sum of its Confederate flag wavers. While it would be cliché to say that being Southern is a state of mind, it is indisputable that self-identification generally is an integral part of defining what it means to be from the South.

* * *

Now, what defines youth? That is arguably an easier answer, as age is defined more literally and confined to linear time.

The Center for Information and Research on Civic Learning and Engagement (CIRCLE), an institute within the Tisch Center for Civic Life at Tufts University that focuses on "young people in the United States, especially those who are marginalized or disadvantaged in political life,"[5] considers young people to be between eighteen and twenty-nine years old.[6] This is the same age range used by pollsters at *Gallup*, *Pew*, and *Five*

---

5   "About CIRCLE," CIRCLE, last accessed October 6, 2019, https:// civicyouth.org/about-circle/.

6   Youth Voting, CIRCLE, last accessed October 6, 2019, https://civicyouth.org/quick-facts/youth-voting/.

Thirty Eight.[7] If we broaden the scope to include all Millennials and Generation Z'ers, then "young people" could stretch to those born as early as 1981.[8] While I tried to look into the youngest possible activist, the stories in this book generally follow the eighteen to twenty-nine guideline.

Beyond the literal understanding of being a young person, there is something to the notion that youth is also a state of mind. The idea of youth coincides with the idea of constantly learning and making mistakes. To be young is to see the world in a way that those who came before do not. Young people are naïve, and many of us do not understand the horrors we face.

While we are empathetic, many of us do not see how people different than us live (in this way we are like some older adults), and as a result we stumble in trying to find common ground. We also tend to discount the wisdom of those who came before

7   See, e.g., Lydia Saad, "Both Parties' Voters Are Keyed Up for Midterm Elections," *Gallup*, September 27, 2018, https://news.gallup.com/poll/243173/parties-voters-keyed-midterm-elections.aspx; "Little Partisan Agreement on the Pressing Problems Facing the U.S.," *Pew Research Center*, October 15, 2018, https://www.people-press.org/2018/10/15/little-partisan-agreement-on-the-pressing-problems-facing-the-u-s/#most-voters-see-high-stakes-for-outcome-of-midterm-elections; Geoffrey Skelley, "Young Voters Might Actually Show Up At The Polls This Year," *FiveThirtyEight,* October 16, 2018, https://fivethirtyeight.com/features/young-voters-might-actually-show-up-at-the-polls-this-year/.

8   Michael Dimock, "Defining generations: Where Millennials end and Generation Z begins." *Pew Research Center*, January 17, 2019, https://www.pewresearch.org/fact-tank/2019/01/17/where-millennials-end-and-generation-z-begins/.

us, and allow our ego to disregard the shoulders of progress on which we stand. We may be selfish, and we may criticize the progress-makers that came before for not moving fast enough—a product of our youth that must be acknowledged.

Young folks have the leg up, however, in our tendency to try again. Whether we are stubbornly trying to convince our parents to give us permission to do something new, or we are tediously trying to find our way through high school, college, or just early adulthood, young folks are unwavering in our perseverance. We have a lot of energy and have not lost the desire to keep trying until we get our way. As a result, young organizers who are given the resources and the platform can learn faster, empathize harder, and get shit done at a more efficient pace.

Concurrently, being older means understanding that those who come after see the world in a way that those before could not imagine. As a Millennial, I will never understand what it is like to grow up not remembering 9/11, like those born in Generation Z. My parents will never understand what it is like to grow up with the threat of a school shooting. My grandparents never understood what it was like to know a country where school segregation was always illegal. Youth brings a new perspective. In the South, the perspective of a defiant younger generation propelled the region through its most trying times. As we continue this journey toward progress, there is no better group of people to listen and to learn from.

There is no common Southerner and there is no common young person.

Like all cultures, Southern culture is not monolithic and requires a wide view to understand what it means to qualify. The people I met with come from different paths to claiming their identity as Southern people, though all are generally dedicated to the cause to claim the narrative of the common Southerner, and especially the common young Southerner.

You will meet:

- Dana Sweeney, a twenty-five-year-old community activist and organizer based in Montgomery, Alabama.

- Arekia Bennett, the twenty-four-year-old Executive Director of Mississippi Votes based in Jackson, Mississippi.

- Raymond Partolan, a twenty-six-year-old undocumented person and immigration activist living in Atlanta, Georgia.

- Joey Wozniak, the twenty-six-year-old Managing Partner of civic engagement organization Mile 22, and Raymond's roommate.

- Megan Newsome, a twenty-three-year-old astrophysicist from Jacksonville, Florida.

- Helen Frink, a twenty-five-year-old community organizer born, raised, and refusing to leave Baton Rouge, Louisiana.

- Charlie Bonner, the twenty-three-year-old Virginian but Texan-at-heart organizing around progressive activism in Austin, Texas.

- Zoe Williamson, the twenty-one-year-old civic engagement activist from the small town of St. Francisville, Louisiana.

Occasionally you will hear from me, a twenty-four-year-old reluctant transplant to Washington, DC from Shreveport, Louisiana. In this story, I am one of the only people who does not live full-time in the South anymore. Though a self-identified, boldly proclaimed Southerner, the journey to my Southerness necessitated considerable self-exploration. Sure, we are Southern, but what does that mean in the larger progressive movement?

What defines being young and being Southern requires self-identification, but self-identification requires an understanding of oneself.

CHAPTER 2

THE STORY OF SELF

So, bless my heart and bless yours, too
I don't know where I'm gonna go
Don't know what I'm gonna do.

- ALABAMA SHAKES, "HOLD ON"

In August 2016, I left home.

Yes, I am still currently a resident of Louisiana (I live there while I am a student). I knew that after that summer, however, everything would be different. I was leaving for Mexico City to embark on a Fulbright scholarship and applying for law schools. Would I be the same person?

I have only ever lived full-time in Louisiana, and by summer 2016, I knew that my calling was to come back and invest in the place that had so invested in me. But now that I would be spending time in other places, I was afraid of losing the person I'd become in exchange for something else. Would I be better, or would I be worse?

Would leaving home cause me to never come back?

That same summer, I attended a student leadership conference hosted by The Andrew Goodman Foundation, a national organization whose mission is to make young voices and votes a powerful force in democracy. I had been a student ambassador for the AGF for two years. After graduating, I was asked to attend and give advice to other students who were entering the program. I was commissioned to help facilitate the "Story of Self," a session where we would teach students how to utilize their own stories to encourage their peers to get involved in the political process by voting and registering to vote.

My only problem: the entire process of telling one's "Story of Self" involved telling your personal story, and I hate talking about myself.

(Don't let this book fool you—writing about myself in this book was the most difficult part of the writing process.)

* * *

I spent my entire life making my story feel more palatable to other people, ashamed of what people might think if they knew that my family moved houses every other year when we couldn't afford to stay, or that I had eleven siblings because of a complicated family tree, or that neither of my parents finished college. I was never confident enough to tell people what I had come from.

Moreover, I did not know myself very well at that time in my life. I just turned twenty-one and graduated from LSU, and I was about to embark on a journey that my North Louisiana childhood could only dream about. I also did not know who I was outside of the life I had planned for myself, while facing a lot of unplanned adventures ahead.

Teaching others how to tell their "Story of Self" required learning how to tell my own.

I sat down and started to learn. Nadia, my co-facilitator for the session and a mentor to me, provided me with the instructions that we would give the students. "Each of us has a story that can move others to action," the instructions prompted. "Public leaders . . . engage people in interpreting why they should change their world (their motivation) and how they can act to change it (their strategy)." I was instructed to think about the "challenge, choice, and outcome" that comprised the plot of my Story of Self. The goal of the session, modeled from a similar tool created by progressive training center New Organizing Institute, was to turn "values into action through stories."

Yikes. I had nothing.

Sure, I had a story, but how could my story possibly move anyone to do anything? And my *motivations?* I really did not think I had any credibility to call anyone to action. But I was asked to do this, and I was grateful to help in anyway I could.

I needed to think of something. I typed up a few quick points in the Notes App on my iPhone. A few minutes and about fifty words later, I had something. I'd scribbled down my challenges, choices, and outcomes, or at least what I thought sounded good enough. I figured that I would wing it for the presentation.

Challenge: racism, growing up with micro-aggressions, and seeing first hand the effect of injustices in daily life (rural childhood: all white schools, confederate flag)

Choice: go into public service, discover a specific path to alleviating theseinjustices (my calling: civic engagement, community organizing foundthrough President Obama's The Audacity of Hope)

Outcome: decision to become an ambassador, decision to go to law school, decision to start an on-campus organization that focused on civic engagement and the results of that (higher education, ID bill)

A few weeks later, I arrived at the conference.

In the middle of the woods near Mahwah, New Jersey, I stood in front of no more than thirty strangers (it felt like thirty thousand). Somehow I was supposed to teach them what I hadn't completely learned myself.

I had given speeches before—just months before, I introduced President Bill Clinton at a rally in Baton Rouge in front of thousands—and here I was in front of a couple dozen teenagers, shaken. I never told anyone *why* I did what I did, or for whom, because I did not think it mattered or that anyone would care. I had never shared my Story of Self.

I stood up with Nadia, who began the session by introducing the students to the topic. It came time to introduce my Story of Self, to demonstrate to the students how to convince others of the power of one's Story of Self.

If I could only convince myself.

* * *

"My childhood was littered with Confederate flags in my neighborhood," I began slowly, trying to remember the stupid notes that I hastily scribbled on my phone. I'd never really spoken to anyone about that before.

Challenge.

I wished I had prepared myself better. "We were the only Black family in my neighborhood for awhile, and I felt isolated sometimes. I went to schools with people who didn't look like me and it shaped how I interacted with the world."

Choice.

I went on for several more minutes, talking about my desire to become a lawyer so that I could change the world, and use what I learned working as a student ambassador. The audience looked receptive, so I kept going.

Outcome.

I talked about the story of Andrew Goodman, who with James Cheney and Mickey Schwerner was killed by the KKK while trying to register Black voters in Mississippi. Their story is my story, I explained. The values that they died for, we have to live for, and we have to continue to do the work to ensure that everyone has equal access to the vote.

The whole thing lasted about five minutes, some of the longest five minutes of my life. For some reason, I received a standing ovation.

* * *

The idea of the Story of Self is to use your personal history to move people to action, to show people that if one person can do it then they can, too. Underlying this goal is self-discovery. To tell our story, we need to learn our story, reckon with our story, and stop being afraid of our story. We may find that other people have a similar story, or that your unique history qualifies you to act or speak with a different authority. We may discover a part of ourselves that we did not understand before, or find a new lesson in retelling a story already told. Storytelling challenges us to learn and act.

Storytelling also reveals common threads.

That moment of sharing my Story of Self induced a lot of anxiety, but also a deep desire to know whom to give credit for the creation of my story. Speaking about the confederate flags in my neighborhood sparked an interest in understanding what other parts of my history were checkered by vestiges of the past.

About a year after first telling my Story of Self, I finally decided to figure it out. Telling my Story for the first time, I realized that my own story was but living history. According to Ances-try.com, my family's roots in North Louisiana go back more than one hundred years, all in the South since before the Civil War. Felik Thompson was born in Ouachita, Louisiana, about an hour away from my hometown. His World War I Draft Registration Cards indicated that he was born on June 5, 1880. His wife, Lizzie Thompson, was born circa 1888. Felik and Lizzie's parents were all likely born before the start of the Civil War, in Mississippi and Georgia. Felik and Lizzie had seven children, including a daughter named Onie Thompson. Onie Thompson gave birth to a girl who got married and became Onie Richardson, who gave birth to my father, Arthur Richardson. In the backdrop of where my family comes from, I discovered a part of who I am.

My experience with Confederate flags is but a sentence in a longer history of a family raised in the Deep South during the Antebellum, Civil War, Jim Crow, and into the present. I can only imagine what my family encountered living in the backdrop of immense racial peril in the Deep South.

There is a living memory running a through line from my hometown of Shreveport, Louisiana that goes about an hour east into Monroe, Louisiana into the home of Felik and Lizzie Thompson. On the way, you'll find a prototypical Southern history. Between 1877 and 1950, when my great-great grand-parents lived and raised children in the city of Monroe,, the highest number of lynchings occurred in Ouachita Parish (where Monroe is located).[9] In the 1960s, right around the time that my father was born, high school students and young members of various civil rights organizations in Monroe led the charge against the active chapters of the White Citizens Council and the Ku Klux Klan during the Civil Rights Movement.[10]

* * *

In the South, unearthing our collective Story of Self requires a real reckoning.

While the discovery process looks different for every person, the skeleton of the task is very much the same. Depending on who we are, identifying what we are looks different; if you Black, for example, you may have little issue understanding the implications of our region's history with racial apartheid. And self-identification is undoubtedly an imperative, because we cannot reach our collective goals without knowing first who we all are individually.

---

9   "Lynching in America: Confronting the Legacy of Racial Terror: SUPPLEMENT: Lynchings by County," Equal Justice Initiative, Third Edition, https://eji.org/sites/default/files/lynching-in-america-third-edition-summary.pdf.

10 Evan Faulkenbury, "'Monroe is Hell': Voter Purges, Registration Drives, and the Civil Rights Movement in Ouachita Parish, Louisiana," *Louisiana History: The Journal of the Louisiana Historical Association*, Vol. 59, No. 1 (Winter 2018), pp. 40-66.

The movement for progress, however, additionally requires the development of a collective identity which recognizes both what the South is and what it could be. Our "challenge, choice, and outcome," is necessarily tied.

The challenge: we are Southern, our history encompasses indescribable evil, and we want to tell our story in a way that confronts, explores, and reckons with that fact.

The choice: Refuse to ignore the indescribable evil, and come to terms with our connection with the inescapable truth.

The outcome (we hope): reconciliation, reparation, and moving forward on a better path toward a more inclusive South.

Once you first tell your Story of Self, you realize that the story needed to be told. For me, the fear of telling my own story stems from the fear of how my story will be received. I am deeply afraid of being ridiculed, and afraid that I am not strong enough to withstand criticism. Telling the world my personal background feels like a cost that may be too high.

For many people in the South, the refusal to tell our story demonstrates a deep denial and shame of the past. There is a desire and a political prerogative to keep our Story of Self untold. What does it mean to point out that our region has never led the country in education or healthcare rates or that thousands of monuments to the Confederacy still litter the region, after all?

Those who seek to maintain an air of comfort and status quo understand that once the story is told, it cannot be untold; progress will be forced by inability to turn away from the truth of what we are.

The refusal to tell the Story only serves as stronger support for the necessity to share as loud and wide as possible. The moment we complete the development of our collective Story of Self, our story of a region starving for change and reconciliation, will be the moment that we can truly mark our first step toward that goal.

This does not mean we make generalizations about who we are. Instead, our Story of Self recognizes the region as rigid, colorful, but incomplete mosaic, comprised of individuals and cultures, and a history that needs serious confrontation. Our job in developing our Story of Self is to tell a story untold and offer lessons therefrom.

* * *

Fortunately, the call to action is not lost on the young.

In 2019, I attended the fifth student leadership conference held by The Andrew Goodman Foundation. This time we were not in the woods, instead taking over part of the campus at Montclair State University in the hilly, suburban Montclair, New Jersey.

Students from across the country, as young as 18, attended the conference; I presented on organizing tactics, but I also used the time to observe the younger students, particularly those from the South. With a few post-grad years behind me, I watched these young folks contemplate the most difficult tasks of their time (How do we get rid of white supremacy in the age of President Donald Trump? How do we talk to people in this polarizing age?).

I watched a student from Florida, 19-year-old Rebecca Diaz, receive an award for standing toe-to-toe with Miami election officials decades her senior, to demand that they provide for Miami Dade College students to early vote on their campuses (a photo of which landed her in the *Miami Herald*). I watched as students insisted that their peers recognize their correct gender pronouns, debated the efficacy of democracy, and agreed to disagree on the merits of talking to their Trump-supporting family members. Most importantly, I noticed young people craving for change, and waiting on people to take their ideas for change seriously.

For young people seeking progress in 2019, the development of the collective Story of Self is already taking hold. The task for all of us is ensuring that the story is told.

* * *

My own Story of Self is incomplete. It's not enough to say that I am a resident of Louisiana. Louisiana is my home and the place that I still call home—as far as I am concerned, I am just passing through other places. I count myself among the young folks whose stories I feel so compelled to tell throughout this book—I am often far away from home, but moved to speak loudly in support of a more complete understanding of the South.

Storytelling is but an attempt at reconciliation; perhaps telling this story is my selfish attempt at apologizing to my home for not spending nearly enough time investing in its well being. Our larger attempt at reconciliation as Southerners begins with understanding who we are and who we can be; coming to peace with and ultimately sharing our truth in the hopes that we can move forward.

CHAPTER 3

ENOUGH

The civil rights movement leaders of the 1960s had no idea that school-shooting survivors from one of the most southern points in the U.S. would lean on their teachings to power a modern nonviolent movement to end gun violence.

-EMMA GONZÁLEZ, TIME

There are certain moments that propel people into action. Moments that shake you to your core and cause you to rethink your preconceived notions.

For young folks, those moments have shaped and defined the course of our lives.

For young Southern folks, those moments have contributed to great steps toward change and progress. As Southerners, we are faced with constant images of great oppression and injustice, and presented with the idea that resistance is futile. It would be natural to assume that this constant bombardment of terror leads to desensitization. And often, that is the case—one may grow apathetic because they are in a position to ignore the pain, or because the barriers blocking the path to change are virtually impassable. Once the disillusionment sets in, it's impossible to see a pathway toward change.

Sometimes you decide to dream for more.

That decision manifests in ways large and small. When I was in high school, I felt charged to action by the reelection of President Barack Obama. It was 2012 and I was just shy of eighteen. I saw the political climate shifting before my eyes.

Like any other high school senior, I was trying to figure out what I wanted to do, and I found that calling in the 2012 election of President Obama. The vitriol that he experienced affected me personally; it felt like the same rhetoric that I experienced as a Black person who occupied a lot of predominantly white spaces—that constant feeling of not belonging.

I read *The Audacity of Hope* like an instruction manual. Obama was just like me, I thought. Though he wasn't a

Southerner (for me at the time, that gave him a few points in his favor), he knew how it felt to feel in constant search for your identity as a Black person and a nontraditional student. He casually studied history, like I casually studied people in history, both of us searching for patterns and trying to find solutions to the problems we perceived. He even has half siblings that he barely knows, just like me. President Obama refused to cede ground, so neither would I. Those years defined the course of the rest of my young career as a student activist.

* * *

Sometimes you merely decide to dream for more. But for much of the time, there comes a point when enough is enough.

When a school shooter took seventeen lives on Valentines Day in 2018 at Marjory Stoneman Douglas High School, young people across the state of Florida, and the region as a whole, came to their sense of civic duty through exacerbation, not mere dreams. The lives of fourteen students and three faculty members were snuffed out by a shooter who had evidence of mental illness and an automatic rifle.[11] The

---

11 Bart Jansen, "Florida shooting suspect bought gun legally, authorities say," *USA Today*, February 15, 2018, https://www. usatoday.com/story/news/2018/02/15/florida-shooting-suspect-bought-gun-legally-authorities-say/340606002/.

tragedy reminded the world of the brutality of gun violence in the United States.

The South in particular grappled with the reality of mass gun violence in the region in the wake of the massacre at Marjory Stoneman Douglas High. Fresh on the collective memory included the shooting in Charleston, South Carolina—killing nine Black churchgoers in congregation; Sutherland, Texas, killing twenty-six people attending Bible study; Pulse Nightclub, in Orlando, Florida, killing forty-nine people for being themselves. Meanwhile, popular support for gun control measures in the South still sat at forty-nine percent shortly before the shooting at Marjorie Stoneman Douglas.[12] Movement on gun control legislation remains stagnant, and stakeholders cannot seem to muster the political will or courage to meaningfully acknowledge the problem.

After Majority Stoneman Douglas, young folks in the South decided that this time would be different.

The students of Majority Stoneman Douglas decided to take matters into their own hands, eventually becoming the faces of the national gun control movement and forming one of the

12 For a view of public support for gun control and gun rights by region, see "Public Views About Guns," *Pew Research Center*, last accessed October 6, 2019, https://www.people-press.org/2017/06/22/public-views-about-guns/#region.

largest youth-led gun control movements in the country. Even as they laid the groundwork for March for Our Lives, thousands of students engaged in a national walk out one month after the shooting to display a unified message: enough.

On the day of the National March for Our Lives, students across the country led thousands in their own regions to demand gun control while the Marjory Stoneman Douglas students rallied more than 800,000 people in Washington, D.C.[13] I helped register young people to vote that day during the rally; the tremendous impact this movement would have was evident. Today, students still lead March for Our Lives local chapters across the country.[14]

The activism reverberated, and student organizers across the region heard the rallying cry and noted how the movement affected their own organizing.

"When you as a student, you see that happening . . . you feel like you have to do something to change it and especially . . . on a college campus," Megan Newsome, twenty-three,

---

13 "March for Our Lives Highlights: Students Protesting Guns Say 'Enough Is Enough'," *New York Times*, March 24, 2018. German Lopez, "It's official: March for Our Lives was one of the biggest youth protests since the Vietnam War," *Vox*, March 26, 2018, https://www.vox.com/policy-and-politics/2018/3/26/17160646/march-for-our-lives-crowd-size-count.

14 "Find A Chapter," March for Our Lives, last accessed October 6, 2019, https://marchforourlives.com/chapters/.

told me. Megan was a researcher and former student at the University of Florida, where she led campus voting rights organizing for The Andrew Goodman Foundation as an ambassador. Now pursuing her PhD in astrophysics at the University of California in Santa Barbara, Megan worked and studied at the University of Florida during the Parkland shooting. While she recruited students in her efforts to increase civic engagement on campus, she witnessed the effect of the Parkland shooting in igniting other students to participate in civic engagement activism.

"You know that other MSD students [attend school with you] and they're . . . depending and relying on you and begging you to go vote and [be] involved," she said. "It . . . makes you want to be involved a little bit more."

Organizers on other college campuses saw this effect, as well. Zöe Williamson, a twenty-one-year-old graduate and former campus organizer and Andrew Goodman ambassador at Louisiana State University, saw how incoming college freshmen sought avenues to get involved in the political process in the wake of the MSD shooting. According to Zöe, many students did not know how to participate, so they would be drawn to any opportunity to learn that they came across.

She tapped into those students' desire to understand the political process by registering them to vote and recruiting many of them in her own voting rights work. As a result, more than 100 student members joined the university's on-campus civic engagement organization, Geaux Vote LSU.

"All of the students that I recruited asked me how they could get involved first," Zöe explained. "I think similar to me, they saw that . . . change wasn't going to happen in our state unless students had a voice and students were able to vote in the [2018 midterm] election."

* * *

The movement for better gun policies is not the only national movement that has taken hold in the South. A new generation, faced with the reality of a changing climate and an uncertainty for the future habitability of an increasingly dying Earth are standing up across the world to advocate for policies which mitigate the effects. The Sunrise Movement, an environmental justice group started by high school kids who helped author the Green New Deal, is a prominent example of young leaders at the forefront of the movement.

The Sunrise Movement and other environment groups took roots in cities across the region, as young Southerners face the particularly perilous challenge of a warming Gulf of Mexico and eroding Gulf Coast. The young South is forcing the region to face the music of the realities of climate change, as a bleak economy compounds the perils of climate change that threaten the future of the region.

The South is one of the most vulnerable regions for the effects of climate change, due to high poverty levels and an increasing number of natural disasters from rising sea levels along the Gulf of Mexico. The effects will be felt most by the present and future generations. Scientists estimate that the South will face some of the greatest economic losses from climate change by the end of the century.[15]

This fact is not lost on young Southern activists, who are seeking to bring climate change to the forefront of the political stage. In 2018, a group of teenage activists from across the country formed the US Youth Climate Strike, which organized hundreds of youth-led protests on May 3, 2019 to promote the Green New Deal and other climate change mitigation policies.[16] On the day of the Youth Climate Strike, young Southern folks showed up, organizing more than a dozen demonstrations across the South. Isabelle Hope's reflection on the events encompasses the defiance felt by young Southerners taking a stance on climate change. A student at the University of Alabama and a Youth Climate

15   Solomon Hsiang et al, "Estimating economic damage from climate change in the United States," *Science Magazine* 356, No. 6345, June 30, 2017, https://science.sciencemag.org/content/356/6345/1362.
16   U.S. Youth Climate Strike, last accessed October 6, 2019, https://www.youthclimatestrikeus.org/.

Strike organizer for the state, she described to *AL.com*: "Alabama is known for being slow to change. That is not acceptable anymore."[17]

* * *

Back in 1992, a lesser-known Stacey Abrams must have felt a similar defiance when she brought the organizing efforts surrounding police brutality to Atlanta, Georgia. In April 1992, riots erupted over the course of five days in Los Angeles in response to the acquittal of the officers who brutally beat Rodney King. As *NPR* recounted, the officers' acquittal and subsequent reaction, which resulted in more than $1 billion in property damage and more than 2,000 people injured, "ignited a national conversation about racial and economic disparity and police use of force that continues today."[18]

That June, then eighteen-year-old Stacey Abrams founded Students for African-American Empowerment with

---

17 Dennis Pillion, "Young Alabamians push for action on climate change," *AL.com*, March 15, 2019, https://www.al.com/news/2019/03/young-alabamians-push-for-action-on-climate-change.html. Ang Li, "'It Will Be Too Late for My Generation.' Meet the Young People Organizing a Massive Climate Change Protest," *TIME*, March 14, 2019, https://time.com/5550823/climate-change-protest-schoolchildren/.

18 Anjuli Sastry and Karen Grigsby Bates, "When LA Erupted In Anger: A Look Back At The Rodney King Riots," *NPR*, April 26, 2017, https://www.npr.org/2017/04/26/524744989/when-la-erupted-in-anger-a-look-back-at-the-rodney-king-riots.

fellow college students in Atlanta.[19] According to the *Atlanta Journal-Constitution's* reporting at the time, the students led the protests in Atlanta following the Rodney King verdicts.[20] This included the public burning of the Georgia flag, at the time emblazoned with the Confederate symbol, on the steps of the Georgia capitol.[21] They faced threats, but did what they thought was right in the wake of a tragic injustice. As fellow SAEE founder, then-twenty-one-year-old Kevin Donalson recalled at the time, "When you step into a situation like this, you have to be willing to give your all."[22]

Over in Virginia, the Unite the Right Rally in 2017 woke up the Virginia residents and students at the progressive-leaning University of Virginia alike. Though generally left-leaning politically, the Charlottesville riots forced a reckoning with the implications of white supremacists storming the community.

During a demonstration, white supremacist groups descended upon the small college town of Charlottesville,

---

19 Nicole Goodkind, "Stacey Abrams burned the Georgia state flag in 1992 to protest confederate imagery and doesn't regret it," *Newsweek*, Oct. 23, 2018, https://www.newsweek.com/stacey-abrams-flag-burning-georgia-confederate-flag-1184153.

20 John Blake, "What Stacey Abrams said about burning the Georgia flag in 1992," *AJC*, June 27, 1992, https://www.ajc.com/news/state--regional-govt--politics/what-stacey-abrams-said-about-burning-the-georgia-flag-1992/tzTgPB8pB7VX7PmyylqoXK/.

21 Ibid.

22 Ibid.

Virginia to protest the city's plans to remove a statue of Robert E. Lee in downtown Charlottesville.[23] According to writer Benjamin Wallace-Wells of the *New Yorker*, sixteen-year old Zyhana Bryant actually prompted the city's decision, as she organized and delivered a petition to the Charlottesville City Council to have the monument removed.[24]

The movement to take down confederate monuments in Charlottesville echoed efforts across the South to remove memorials to The Lost Cause, including the successful effort to take down a Confederate monument in my hometown of Shreveport, Louisiana.[25] The Southeastern region still boasts more than 1,000 monuments to the Confederacy, according to the Southern Poverty Law Center.[26] The widespread movement to remove them gained speed after South Carolina's

23 Brandon Griggs, "Protests over Confederate statue shake Charlottesville, Virginia," *CNN*, May 15, 2017, https://www.cnn.com/2017/05/15/us/charlottesville-lee-monument-spencer-protests-trnd/index.html.

24 Benjamin Wallace-Wells, "The Fight Over Virginia's Confederate Monuments," *New Yorker*, November 27, 2017, https://www.newyorker.com/magazine/2017/12/04/the-fight-over-virginias-confederate-monuments.

25 For a detailed history of the confederate monument in Caddo Parish at a parish courthouse, see the federal district court's decision to uphold its removal at *Shreveport Chapter #237 of United Daughters of the Confederacy v. Caddo Par. Comm'n*, 331 F. Supp. 3d 605, 609 (W.D. La. 2018), aff'd sub nom. *Shreveport Chapter #237 of United Daughters of Confederacy v. Caddo Par. Comm'n*, 756 F. App'x 460 (5th Cir. 2019).

26 "Whose Heritage? Public Symbols of the Confederacy," Southern Poverty Law Center, February 1, 2019, https://www.splcenter.org/20190201/whose-heritage-public-symbols-confederacy.

decision to remove confederate monuments in the wake of the shooting at Emanuel African Methodist Episcopal Church.[27]

The movement in Charlottesville brought a violent confrontation between white supremacists, anti-fascist counter-protestors, and a bewildered community. In what the *Washington Post* described as an effort "meant to evoke similar marches of Hitler Youth and other ultra-right nationalist organizations of the past century," the protest brought hundreds of white supremacists and Nazi sympathizers brandishing pitchforks and shouting "You will not replace us."[28]

The rally went through the night and reconvened the following afternoon. Counter-protester Heather Heyer was killed in the ensuing riots, and many others injured.[29] The "Summer of Hate" cost Charlottesville taxpayers approximately $1.4 million and much more in emotional losses.[30]

---

27 Ibid.

28 Joe Heim, "Recounting a day of rage, hate, violence and death," *Washington Post*, Aug. 4, 2017, https://www.washingtonpost.com/graphics/2017/local/charlottesville-timeline/?noredirect=on&utm_term=.e455f20110ee.

29 Ibid.

30 "2017 Unite the Right rally cost state police $916K," *Daily Progress*, Sept. 21, 2018, https://www.dailyprogress.com/news/local/unite-the-right-rally-cost-state-police-k/article_cd8b01b0-bde3-11e8-8a80-d7db0903376a.html.

In response to the Unite the Right rally, University of Virginia students took charge of the reconciliation process; the Black Student Alliance started with proposed a series of demands to the university.[31] Among the demands included removing the remaining confederate plaques from the university, acknowledging a gift given to the university by the KKK in 1921, and working to increase the population of the university so that the racial diversity of the school reflects that of the rest of the state.[32]

The UVA Student Council unanimously passed a resolution supporting the demands, forcing the university's administration to respond.[33] "I know it doesn't solve institutional problems . . . but I think the least it does is make me feel like I have a right to be here, that my friends and I have a right to be here," college junior Rawda Fawaz said to the *Cavalier Daily* of the demands.[34]

The young folks leading the effort to confront the University of Virginia's, and the town of Charlottesville by extension, uncomfortable history is a lesson in steadfast reconciliation

---

31 Thomas Roades, "Student Council endorses Black Student Alliance demands after heated session," *Cavalier Daily*, August 30, 2017, https://www.cavalierdaily.com/article/2017/08/student-council-endorses-black-student-alliance-demands-after-heated-session.

32 Ibid.

33 Ibid.

34 Ibid.

for us all. At the University of Virginia, the Black students who already had to face this history every day decided that they had enough of people choosing to ignore it.

* * *

To be sure, deciding that enough is enough comes at a cost. Choosing to share one's trauma means healing in public—another personal sacrifice made by young activists in their efforts to save us all. The trauma already forces young people to grow up much faster than they should have to, and the compounding public pressure makes their sacrifice all the more astounding.

As *The Nation* reported, Black students at the University of Virginia had to receive counselling services for the trauma they suffered from the aftermath of the Unite the Right rally.[35] One student remarked, "At the end of the day, nothing could have prepared me for the real fear of dying. We were the first people to have an altercation with this group . . . No one really knew how violent they intended to be."[36]

According to *The Nation*, UVA counselors organized a group crisis intervention session for the students who protested the

---

35   Alexis Gravely, "At the University of Virginia, Black Students Are Still Recovering From August 11," *The Nation*, May 16, 2018, https://www.thenation.com/article/at-the-university-of-virginia-black-students-are-still-recovering-from-august-11/.

36   Ibid.

Unite the Rally, as well as other support groups.[37] However, students reported that the short-term crisis intervention did not address the long-term trauma that they would suffer from as a result of the event.[38]

Likewise, many students from Majorie Stoneman Douglas speak openly about the post-traumatic stress disorder they suffer from as a result of the shooting. The state of Florida has spent an estimated $69 million in counseling after the shooting at MSD.[39] Nevertheless, students carry the long-term trauma of the event even as they put themselves in the public eye. A year after the shooting, two students who survived the shooting at MSD committed suicide, prompting calls for greater mental health support within the Parkland community.[40] Speaking to the New York Times, a fifteen-year-old survivor of the shooting remarked, "Like, I want to have closure. But I don't know if it's attainable."[41]

---

37 Ibid.

38 Ibid.

39 Elizabeth Koh, "Florida spent $69M on mental health after Parkland but didn't mention suicide prevention," *Tampa Bay Times*, March 27, 2019, https://www.tampabay.com/florida-politics/2019/03/27/florida-spent-69m-on-mental-health-after-parkland-but-almost-nothing-for-suicide-prevention-ptsd/.

40 Skyler Swisher, "Parkland teen suicides prompt calls for more mental health funding," *Sun Sentinel*, March 29, 2019, https://www.sun-sentinel.com/news/florida/fl-ne-school-mental-health-funding-20190329-story.html.

41 Michael Barbaro, "The Parkland Students, One Year Later," The Daily by the New York Times, February 14, 2019, https://www.nytimes.com/2019/02/14/podcasts/the-daily/parkland-stoneman-douglas-school-shooting.html.

* * *

Young people channel their pain into tangible calls to action—an action which demands our respect and listening ear. For young Southern activists, this includes carrying the generational trauma brought by the history of the region, in addition to the trauma being wrought by current events.

When our emotional limits are challenged, we rise to the occasion, because there is no other choice. While that does not mean ignoring the pain, it does mean that we are confronting the cause of the pain with direct action, be it racism, environmental justice, or mass violence. What becomes problematic is deciding who must step forward when the going gets tough.

CHAPTER 4

OUT OF THE SHADOWS

———

It's been too hard living, but I'm afraid to die
'Cause I don't know what's up there, beyond the sky
It's been a long, a long time coming
But I know a change gonna come, oh yes it will.

— SAM COOKE

By all accounts, John Lewis was resolute as he stepped onto the picket line along the Edmund Pettus Bridge.

At only twenty-five years old, he seemed to realize something that many vulnerable people seeking change have to find out on their own: stepping up often means putting your life, and your livelihood, on the line. Later, on the fiftieth anniversary of Bloody Sunday, John Lewis would remark, "I thought I saw death."[42]

All notions of fairness would indicate that forcing the most vulnerable to show their vulnerabilities is a quite unfair compromise. It makes little sense that the very people who are fighting for better lives have to risk their lives to do so. But we see it in every movement; those who have everything to lose simultaneously risk everything.

Deciding to confront danger for the greater goals of your cause is a tragedy of being a young Southern activist. From LGBTQ rights to environmental justice, countless others have decided to step out of the shadows to tackle the great issues of our time facing the Deep South. Young people literally put their lives on the line, hoping in great desperation that someone will see their suffering and be moved to act.

What's worse, these acts of standing on the front lines to confront injustice do not always occur by the will of the person forced out of the shadows.

The violent murder of twenty-one-year-old Muhlaysia Booker sparked national outrage about the damning rates of violence

---

42 "John Lewis reflects on Selma: 'I thought I saw death,'" *USA Today*, March 5, 2015, https://www.youtube.com/watch?v=F-DrYRXEqZY.

targeting trans women in the South.[43] A report by the Transgender Law Center found that fifty-eight percent of trans women reported experiencing high levels of stranger violence.[44]

The story of Trayvon Martin, only seventeen years old when George Zimmerman shot and killed him while walking in his Florida neighborhood, sparked a conversation about gun violence toward communities of color. Ten states, five in the South, still have explicit stand-your-ground laws.[45]

No one will ever forget the fourteen high school students who were slain in Parkland, Florida, whose death sparked a worldwide movement on school safety, or the Pulse Nightclub shooting in Orlando, which took the lives of forty-nine people and exposed the great danger marginalized people face in public spaces—at least to those who were not previously paying attention.

The decision to step out of the shadows is a decision to force light on the injustices facing the most vulnerable

43   Emanuella Grinberg, "There's Something Different About the Public Reaction to Muhlaysia Booker's Death," *CNN,* June 3, 2019, https://www.cnn.com/2019/05/29/us/muhlaysia-booker-funeral/index.html.

44   Transgender Law Center, "The Grapevine: A Southern Trans Report," May 2019, http://transgenderlawcenter.org/wp-content/uploads/2019/05/grapevine_report_eng-FINAL.pdf.

45   Self Defense and "Stand Your Ground," National Conference of State Legislatures, July 27, 2018, http://www.ncsl.org/research/civil-and-criminal-justice/self-defense-and-stand-your-ground.aspx.

and disenfranchised. Unfortunately, forcing light on those injustices also results in the involuntarily sacrifice of those being exposed.

* * *

Immigration is among the most pressing issues currently facing our region, and the plight for immigrant rights represents the sacrifice those most vulnerable confront to pursue those rights. The light shone on the immigration crisis is most often facilitated through the involuntary exposure of a vulnerable immigrant community; only after stories of children sleeping on rocks and being denied toothpaste at a facility in the middle of the Texas desert, for example, did many across the country realize the extent of the inhumanity resulting from this country's immigration policies.[46]

Though framed as a national issue, the immigration debate has embroiled the Southeast perhaps more than any other region in the country, save the Southwest. Immigration activists across the region advocate against the separation of families at the border, outdated asylum processes, and

---

46 For one account of the horror, see Meagan Flynn, "Detained migrant children got no toothbrush, no soap, no sleep. It's no problem, government argues," *Washington Post*, June 21, 2019, https://www.washingtonpost.com/nation/2019/06/21/detained-migrant-children-no-toothbrush-soap-sleep/.

brutal racism faced by the migrants who do manage to make their way past the ports of entry.

I am a volunteer interpreter and legal assistant for people seeking asylum, and am always amazed by the stark contrast between immigration policies, migrant culture, and the preconceived notions by fellow Southerners. In summer 2019, I spent a week working in San Antonio, Texas as a volunteer at a family detention center, helping women with their asylum claims. San Antonio boasts one of the most vibrant immigrant communities in the country; the seventh-largest city in the country, more than fourteen percent of San Antonio residents are foreign-born.[47]

Tucked away about an hour outside of this diverse city are some of the largest migrant detention centers in the country. The detention center reminded me of jail, a stark representation of the inhumanity hiding behind relative prosperity.

* * *

In the midst of the involuntary sacrifices made by the unwitting faces of the immigration crisis, there are also those immigrants who voluntarily step into the spotlight to give a face to

---

47 San Antonio's Immigrant Community Data, San Antonio Government, last updated 2018, https://www.sanantonio.gov/humanservices/ImmigrationServices/ImmigrantCommunityData.

the people affected by this crisis. Young undocumented advocates, who may fear deportation or the deportation of their families, make the active decision to reveal their immigration status as a part of the larger movement to change immigration policies. These organizations include United We Dream, an immigration advocacy organization with an online reach of more than four million people and four hundred thousand members—the largest immigrant youth-led organization in the country, according to its website.[48]

Some hope to show that immigrants are just as deserving of human rights as American citizens. The most basic, optimistic hope is that those who deny immigrants' human dignity see their humanity when they realize that immigrants are their neighbors, community members, and colleagues.

I spoke with Raymond Partolan, an undocumented activist raised in Georgia, on how being open about his immigration status is imperative to his activism. Raymond, twenty-six years old, was born in the Philippines but moved to the United States when he was one year old.

Raised in Macon, Georgia, Raymond's family came here legally. He, his father, and his mother had work visas but their legal ability to stay in the United States ended when

---

48 "About UWD," United We Dream, last accessed October 6, 2019, https://unitedwedream.org/about/.

Raymond was ten years old. This is common among many undocumented families; a report by the Center for Migration Studies found that the overwhelming majority of undocumented people living in the United States from 2010 to 2017 became undocumented due to visa overstay.[49] Raymond has been undocumented ever since.

"It's really formed the way that I approach my work and everything that I do," Raymond said to me. In his personal website, aptly named *Outside of the Shadows*, Raymond details the story of his family's journey to the United States and living life as an undocumented person in Georgia.[50] A few years after becoming undocumented, Raymond attempted suicide due to the fear of his immigration status. Only sixteen years old, he took a handful of Tylenol, thinking that life as an undocumented person was not a life worth living.

"I thought that [suicide] was the only way that I was going to be able to relieve myself of the suffering that I was feeling. And so I tried to kill myself. And I remember lying on the ground, in my bathroom, upstairs in my parent's house and deciding, you know, like, what am I doing?" Raymond

---

49 Robert Warren, "US Undocumented Population Continued to Fall from 2016 to 2017, and Visa Overstays Significantly Exceeded Illegal Crossings for the Seventh Consecutive Year," *Center for Migration Studies*, January 16, 2019, https://cmsny.org/publications/essay-2017-undocumented-and-overstays/.

50 You can read it here: https://outsideoftheshadowsblog.wordpress.com.

recounted. "This issue affects me very personally. But I am not in this situation alone. And that's when I decided that I needed to use whatever talents and abilities that I was blessed with to really advocate for other people in my similar situation."

And so he did. Soon after, he began sharing his story publicly and advocating on behalf of immigrant communities. Still a kid, Raymond felt determined to show his small Georgia community what it looked like to be an undocumented person. In college, Raymond undertook independent organizing around higher education issues for immigrant communities, including advocating for scholarships. After college, Raymond worked as an organizer for Asian Americans Advancing Justice. When the DACA program launched in 2012, Raymond's ability to vocalize his status amplified.

By stepping out of the shadows, Raymond continues to stand in defiance against this country's broken immigration system and the stereotypes surrounding undocumented people. Raymond believes that he should eventually have the opportunity to get his green card, but his work won't be over regardless.

"After having personally experienced our immigration system and how unfair it is and how arbitrary it is in a lot of ways, this is something that I see as an issue that affects so many millions of people whether I get my permanent residence or not," Raymond said. "I'm not gonna stop fighting until every single one of these people has a reasonable pathway to citizenship."

As Raymond knows, there are millions of people living in the shadows. Allie Yee, a research fellow for the Institute for Southern Studies, noted in *Facing South* magazine that more than one million undocumented people live in the South.[51] Living as an undocumented person in the United States brings many challenges, including finding work, shelter, and avoiding hostile government authorities. Southern undocumented people face the unique challenge of living near the border but far from a place of understanding on the part of fellow Southerners.

An undocumented person must figure out how to remain undetected with every decision they make in their daily lives. Compound this vigilance with the insidious stereotypes of immigrants stealing jobs and committing crimes, as well as hostility from anti-immigrant community members (who may not know that their neighbor is undocumented) and the added racial hostility of the confederate flag wavers and Southern Pride pronouncers, and there is no wonder why one may decide to simply hide their status.

---

51 Allie Yee, "Three years of DACA: Changing lives of young people in the South," *Facing South,* June 19, 2015, https://www.facingsouth.org/2015/06/three-years-of-daca-changing-lives-of-young-people.

Undocumented people in the South literally live in the shadows.

* * *

The decision to tell one's story in any context is difficult, and often requires significant personal sacrifice.

In addition to the personal risk you may take on, one must consider the risk to family members and close friends. At what point is the sacrifice worth it? And, why do the most vulnerable people have to be the ones to make this sacrifice?

In normal circumstances, putting oneself out there is an inherent risk; it requires confidence (or faking confidence), bucking risk aversion, and deciding that being vulnerable does not outweigh the benefits of telling your story. While one may consider their loved ones tangentially, the calculation to step out of the shadows is ultimately personal; at the end of the day, it is your story to tell, no matter how many people helped write it. The risk of life and livelihood only raises the stakes, and making the decision to stand up despite that risk is undeniably brave.

For Raymond, this meant telling his story in full, to anyone who will listen. As a result, we as his audience get the privilege of understanding the scope of his sacrifice—and why that sacrifice should not be necessary.

Raymond's suicide attempt propelled him to action, which brought him to becoming an activist for his community. As life works, there have been good and bad times, but his decision to live freely as an undocumented person changes lives. His decision to step out of the shadows forces us to realize that he should never have had to face the situation in the first place.

What sort of broken immigration system punishes people for legally arriving to the United States? What sort of broken culture places the blame on immigrants for falling through the gaping cracks of that utterly broken system? It is not fair, and by telling us this story, Raymond forces the rest of us to remember that.

* * *

There is something to be said about facing unjust forces to confront the humanity of its victims.

Realistically, those forces will be unmoved by the reality of the damage they cause, but this display is not just for them. In the South, we would be naïve to think that the same oppressors—whose legacies live on, continuing to fight its Lost Cause of the Confederacy—will change their mind by seeing the extent of the suffering they have called. The oppressors do not see the oppressed as fully human, so reaching out to them may be an aimless goal.

When stepping out of the shadows to confront injustice, we hope to force their hands, as the onlookers are now faced with the reality of just standing by. Fucked as it may be, we aim to reach out to the people who still have the potential to care, and gain support to the cause of equity.

If this is a numbers game, we are not reaching out to active oppressors, but passive supporters. If we can share our vulnerabilities and reach one empathetic soul, then we have pushed this heavy rock one step up the mountain. It is for the victims themselves—a display of pride, a show of strength and resolve despite the barriers dedicated to their oppression. To step out of the shadows is to push yourself and others to stand unashamed.

And what better way is there to force a movement?

* * *

During those dangerous times of the Civil Rights Movement, Black folks would risk their jobs and risk falling prey to the Ku Klux Klan. A young John Lewis, rising from his humble roots, risked his entire future for the cause of human rights in the American South and the end of the apartheid state of Jim Crow.

As you might know, John Lewis did not step back into the shadows after that historic moment. After John Lewis saw death, he eventually saw vindication; among other victories, his instrumental role in the Civil Rights Movement led to the Civil Rights Act of 1964, Voting Rights Act of 1965, and the Fair Housing Act of 1968. The young John Lewis grew up to be Congressman John Lewis, where he remains to this day. He often employs the term "good trouble," understanding from a young age that sometimes fighting for the right thing means creating controversy.

By choosing to step out of the shadows and share his story, he demanded that the world look injustice square in the face and do something about the evil permeating throughout the South.

In 2018, almost ten years after he almost took his own life, Raymond accepted the Hubert H. Humphrey Civil and Human Rights Award from the Leadership Conference on Civil and Human Rights. He accepted the award on behalf of all undocumented people, whose bravery and resilience the Leadership Conference decided to recognize. Raymond stepped out of the shadows into the biggest spotlight of his young life.

"We are here to fight until every single one of the eleven million undocumented people who call this country home has a reasonable pathway to citizenship," he promised in front of a crowd of civil rights activists in Washington, DC—a long way from home in Georgia.

Onward he goes, like the brave young activists upon whose shoulders he stands, out of the shadows and leading us toward progress. If only his sacrifice was unnecessary.

CHAPTER 5

WHAT DO WE DO?

———

A grown child is a dangerous thing.

- ALICE WALKER, THE COLOR PURPLE

The South is a stubborn toddler who keeps putting her hand on a hot stove after her mother tells her to stop.

If you keep putting your hand on the stove, you'll get burned.

The toddler, understanding that putting her hand on the hot burner only leads to a burned hand and another round of punishment, looks at her mother and places her hand on the stove anyway.

By now, the toddler already knows how this story plays out, because she has been here before. Yet she is defiant—it is unclear if she even grasps that she is doing the wrong thing by repeating the same bad act—because she does not like doing what she is told. She finally understands what her mom was trying to protect her from after the last time she puts her hand on the stove, when she really hurts herself and is feeling a lot of pain.

In the South, we continue to live a storied history. Like a defiant toddler, we don't seem to learn the depth of our mistakes until people get hurt. Our past is one of brutal racism, prejudice, and economic disparity, and blazing oppression throughout our region to the most vulnerable.

Our past is still our present. We currently live in the region counted among the lowest quality in education, health, and criminal justice. Racial disparities abound; like a broken record, public leaders decry a lack of "responsibility" and promise change in the same breath.

Problems ostensibly left behind in the days of Jim Crow and the Antebellum are but events repeated. It feels like we are doomed to a Groundhog Day, whereby injustice prevails, enough people become outraged, mass change occurs, those former oppressors resist the change, and repeat.

In the 2010s, we seem to have transitioned into the first phase—injustice prevails by leaps and bounds. From Texas to Virginia, and up to Tennessee and Kentucky, waves of unjust laws and stories of inhumanity permeate the regional and national conscious.

In 2019, Alabama passed a ban on abortion that criminalizes doctors who perform abortions with up to ninety-nine years in prison—the next day, the state executed another man on death row, in seeming contrast to its pro-life propagandizing in the days before.

Scientists warn that climate change along the Gulf Coast will erode the land across Louisiana, Mississippi, and Alabama, as well as the Everglades in Florida—oil companies maintain their foothold in the region.

Thousands of migrants cross through the Texas-Mexico border to seek asylum from their war-torn homes, only to be deported or separated from their families.

States have passed or proposed voting rights laws which impose the risk of criminal penalties on people seeking to register fellow citizens to vote.

Stories of attempted lynchings coupled with riots promoting the former Confederacy rage on.

While injustice is a constant throughout time, this decade has seen injustices the likes of which the South has not seen since the Civil Rights Movement when the KKK led the campaign for white supremacy and terrorized all who got in their way.

* * *

If past is prologue, then we should be looking to the outraged to help us stop this vicious cycle and move our region toward something like progress.

Perhaps we could be looking for the people already at work, ready for the platform by which to expand and create broad change.

As Margaret Renkl noted in the *New York Times*, our focus should turn on "the worried Southerners who didn't leave."[52] The "worried Southerners," those who live and work in the South, who had the opportunity to get out but didn't, are the ones for whom we are looking; the worried Southerners who are concerned about the current state of affairs but may be desensitized to the idea of hope and change.

In particular, those young and making the radical decision to stay and fight back are the worried Southerners I would

---

52 Marget Renkl, Shame and Salvation in the American South, *New York Times*, May 20, 2019, https://www.nytimes.com/2019/05/20/opinion/the-american-south.html.

place my money on. While the worried Southerners who didn't leave on the whole are searching for a way out of the current affairs, the younger generation are the ones with a vision that we can look toward. Moreover, in my experience, those most worried are on the edge of eighteen, figuring out their next steps and wondering if their place is at home or somewhere far away.

Throughout my time listening to and learning about the young people across the region who are dedicated to staying and doing the work, I couldn't stop wondering whether anyone else ever listened to the ideas they have for this place. Sure, we see the students of Marjory Stoneman Douglas on the front cover of magazines, and most people vaguely understand the role college students played in the Civil Rights Movement. There is a general understanding that the youth are our future, and a general hope that younger generations do it better than the generations before were able to accomplish.

Outside of that attention, few invest time or resources into understanding the role that young people can play in stopping this cycle of injustice. As a result, the lessons we can learn from them are lost in the chaos of current events; a sad irony, as people loudly lament that there is no one to turn to.

* * *

After listening to and watching my fellow young Southerners, I did learn several ways we should be working to putting their efforts at the forefront of the larger movement toward progress in the region.

We can first learn to stop underestimating young Southern progressives.

For one, the work on the ground involves constant firefighting. The nature of firefighting means never finding the time to rebuild. One fire is put out, the flames of oppression drowned out by dedication of community organizers, while another fire rages on miles way with no one to pan the flames. Whether working as a lobbyist in a state legislature, an abortion clinic defender, or a community organizer, the constant focus is to resolve the current crisis and prevent the next one.

This necessity means not having the time to build a foundation from which policies can be fomented. This make sense; oppressive policies require keeping the opposition busy and distracted from the larger goal. While activists spent their time protecting clinic defenders from harassment, anti-choice zealots worked to get the right legislators elected to vote on the strictest abortion bill in the country.

Young organizers are slow to tire of the firefight. Young organizers, by way of their inexperience and gun-ho attitudes (and perhaps a bit of optimism that it is possible to change anyone's hearts and minds) are naturally on the frontlines of organizing.

We are the ones who knock on doors, spread the word on social media, and speak out in defiance to our elected officials. We are the ones waiting for someone to finally take us seriously. We are not perfect—many of the people we know and love participate in the very oppression that we protest, and some among us participate in widening gentrification of our communities, for example. But on the whole, we are willing to try and are definitely more willing to learn than the other folks.

To underestimate young Southern progressives, then, is to undermine the movement. The nation does the rest of the region a disservice when it decides to write off those young progressives in the South as delusional or unrealistic. The most effective leaders in the region got their start when they made the personal choice to stay in the fight. Instead, look to their work and their motivations, and ask where you can best be helpful.

We can next learn to start supporting young Southern progressives.

Speaking to Joey Wozniak, the twenty-six-year-old Managing Partner of Mile 22 Associates from Georgia (and

Raymond's roommate), he lamented to me the lack of philanthropic investment into the region: "The impact philanthropic movement doesn't exist in the Southeast."

A report by the National Committee for Responsive Philanthropy and Grantmakers for Southern Progress backs up his concerns. The report, *On Fertile Soil,* found that foundations invested a mere $41 per person in the Black Belt and Mississippi Delta regions between 2010 and 2014, compared to the national average of $451 per person.[53] The report acknowledges what many young organizers in the region see with their own eyes: the nation does not listen to Southerner community organizers, and rarely is money invested in community organizing or policy building.

As the report concludes, "Southern leaders understand what is and is not possible in their communities. They understand what rhetoric can push the boundaries of the possible in a productive way and what rhetoric may push them to the breaking point."[54] A meaningful financial investment in the region would be a literal demonstration of good faith in the folks working to advance the region. If the idea that the crises are a foregone conclusion perpetuate the crises that affect

53 Ryan Schlegel and Stephanie Peng, "As the South Grows: On Fertile Soil," National Committee for Responsive Philanthropy and Grantmakers for Southern Progress, April 4, 2017, https://www.ncrp.org/publication/as-the-south-grows-on-fertile-soil.

54 Ibid.

the South, then the failure to invest in the region only keeps the wheel spinning.

Apart from financial investment, there is little by the way of time investment to young progressives in the region. My own part in telling these stories is to provide a platform to share their mission, but also to demonstrate that there is a deep need for more people to invest in providing a platform to the countless community organizers and activists working on the ground every day.

To be sure, there are many stories told of the scrappy Southerner whose rise to stardom could mark some big political revolution in the region—the *New York Times*' profile of University of Mississippi graduate Allen Coon portrayed "a Liberal" that "wanted to agitate Ole Miss from the inside," by advocating for the removal of the Mississippi state flag. The profile rightfully acknowledged Allen's work as an ally and accomplice, and his journey to combating injustice, but notably failed to center the Black students who led the charge.

These stories are a dime a dozen, and inspiring they may be but comprehensive they are often not. Those stories are often infantilizing, as they identify a problem with the South and resolve that the solution is to learn from the success of others (often read: North). In this effort to show the South a "better way," these stories fail to demonstrate the scope of the work already undertaken. A real, genuine investment from the region and the nation would profile the stories of the clinic defender and the young lobbyist fresh out of college— we are willing to talk if y'all are willing to listen.

Relatedly, we can learn to stop patronizing those who decide to stay.

Any of the young men and women that I spoke to undoubtedly could have left their homes and never come back. Indeed, many considered it, but found that home was where they belonged. What tends to happen, however, is that those who decide to dedicate their careers to the cause of Southern progression find themselves facing criticism from peers (both from home and not) regarding their deliberate choice to not leave the same place they complain about.

But when studies show that the majority of people never leave their home states, why should Southern folks be criticized for doing the same?[55] Those who claim to not understand why progressives stay in the South forget that the South is home for us. Just like any young person in any other part of the country, we would like to stay close to our parents and what we know. More importantly, we would like to invest

---

55   Robert Kelchen and Douglas A. Webber, "Examining the Interstate Mobility of Recent College Graduates," *Educational Researcher*, Vol. 47 No. 3, pp. 213–215 (April 2008).

our talents back where we live, to give back to the place that raised us. Like any other person deciding what to do with the rest of his or her life, eventually we want the place we call home to be worthy of us to live in.

* * *

There is an honor to not leaving your fellow Southerner behind. At a time where political polarization is moving more progressives to the East and West coasts, there is less political capital among progressives than ever before.

Those of us who left have not simply made a personal choice to get away. We have left defenseless the most vulnerable who have no option to get out. In this sense, leaving is not a real option.

There is common sense of obligation in staying. In other words, they stay because there would be no one else to do the work otherwise. Any narrative surrounding the progressive South should acknowledge those who make the active decision to stay and change things, as well as those who have no choice but to stay. Rather, we should thank them for choosing not to leave.

The old adage by English writer George Santayana tells us that those who do not remember the past are condemned to repeat it. The South is not just stuck in the past. Our oppressors condemn us to repeat it, and even those well-meaning are too disillusioned to push back. The one demographic of people who have always refused to push back, however, are those too young to be hopeless. And those of us who are still young and invested in change deserve that our ideas be heard, taken seriously, and invested into.

If the past can teach us anything, it is that the past is not over; the fierceness, passion, and hope of the young is not new. To break the chains, we need to start harnessing that energy more efficiently.

CHAPTER 6

IF NOT ME, THEN WHO?

I am in Birmingham because injustice is here.

- MARTIN LUTHER KING, JR.,

LETTER FROM A BIRMINGHAM JAIL

When Martin Luther King, Jr. wrote Letter from a Birmingham Jail, he probably did not know he would be speaking about a generation of teenagers and twenty-somethings who spend most of their time on their phones.

I like to think that Dr. King was speaking to some distant future, hoping that generations not yet thought of would be called to action, to face injustice when they see it. Maybe he didn't just write his letter and have it snuck out of the Birmingham jail (where he was being held for protesting injustice in the Alabama town along with other members of the Southern Nonviolent Coordinating Committee) just to chastise those white moderates who were getting timid about all the uproar during the campaign in Birmingham.

Maybe Dr. King also sought to preserve the memory of his time in jail to speak to all of us looking to progress the South, and to remind us that progress only stops when we stop working.

At least, he was speaking to me. I want to be home, speak about home, and work on behalf of home because injustice is at home. I want to work on issues that affect my home, and invest in my home. I want others to know the beauty of my home, and the resilience of my home's people.

Like many other young activists who thirst for change in the South, I refuse to cede ground to injustice. I decided that I would dedicate my career to fighting injustice back home in the Deep South, no matter where I am located physically. Whether or not I am physically at my hometown of Shreveport, Louisiana, I am "here," because if I am not here then there is no one else to take my place.

If not me, then who?

This is not a statement of arrogance; there are just not enough young Southerners on the ground to do the work. More importantly, there are not enough people on the ground who both understand the obstacles they are working against and desire to do the work anyway.

In a region where it feels like oppressive results are but a foregone conclusion, even the potential for change requires the public presence of people who refuse to believe that the South's outcomes have to be what they are. Progress, after all, is but a numbers game. Though it may take only one person to start a movement, it takes countless others to sustain it and ensure the movement's success.

The answer to *if not me, then who?* is already known: When a young person is inactive from the cause, there is no one to take their place.

* * *

Many young progressives who do become successful leave their home and never look back; the ones who decide to stay feel like they can never leave.

Zöe Williamson, an organizer in her own right, recognized her obligation to her community early on. At just twenty-one years old, she used her platform as the president of the first college-student run civic engagement organization in Louisiana, Geaux Vote LSU, to implement a voter registration program on LSU's 30,000-student campus. She successfully petition the East Baton Rouge Metro Council to implement a polling location on campus for the 2020 elections, and register more than 2,000 college students to vote (full disclosure: I helped found Geaux Vote LSU in 2015). She is from St. Francisville, Louisiana—a classic, picturesque South Louisiana town of approximately 1,600 people, where the moss grows as fast as the sun rises and sets.

Though a young leader herself, Zöe is looking ahead to future young leaders by training younger students behind her. Now graduated, Zöe resides in Baton Rouge where she is working to re-elect the only Democratic governor in the Deep South, Louisiana Governor John Bel Edwards. While Zöe figures out her next steps—graduate school is certainly in her future, as well as creating her own nonprofit—she remains dedicated to the cause of youth voting rights in Louisiana.

"If I were to leave, I'm the only person who cares about it," she remarked to me. "I'm trying to create a generation of students at LSU who care about it, by giving them all the information [they need] and hopefully a couple of them will care and will actually do the work," she hopes. "But right now if I didn't, there's no one who's gonna fight for it."

If not me, then who? also serves as a caution. The answer to that question could easily be *if not me, then someone with less privilege than me*; or worse, *if not me, then someone with more to lose than me.*

As we previously saw, the common strategy employed in confronting injustice is to give a face, sometimes an unwitting face, into the spotlight to demonstrate the humanity of the cause. This should not have to be. As more people with privilege step away, more of the most vulnerable are forced out of the shadows.

While one should never look to speak on any other group's behalf, one should always step up to stand beside the most vulnerable—and to follow their lead. What would the Civil Rights Movement have been without the clergymen who answered Dr. King's call to join the campaign in Alabama? One of those was a white, twenty-six-year-old Episcopal seminarian, Jonathan Daniels, who was shot gunned to death by an unpaid "special deputy."[56] He took the blast to save a fellow activist, Ruby Sales. Dr. King later said, "One of the most heroic Christian deeds of which I have heard in my entire ministry was performed by Jonathan Daniels."

---

56 For a moving recollection on the life of Jonathan Daniels, see Michael E. Ruane, "Black Civil Rights Activist Recalls White Ally Who Took A Shotgun Blast for Her," *Washington Post*, Aug. 16, 2015, https://www.washingtonpost.com/local/black-civil-rights-activist-recalls-white-ally-who-took-a-shotgun-blast-for-her/2015/08/16/4e562dd8-3b74-11e5-8e98-115a3cf7d7ae_story.html.

If not me, then there are not enough allies in the fight. And since there is no one to take your place, *if not me,* then the most marginalized stand alone.

As someone who left the South full-time but still focuses her work in the region, I am in a peculiar place. I needed to be away because I did not want to regret having stayed forever, but I still feel compelled to supplement the work that is missing on the ground in my absence.

That is probably why, perhaps selfishly, I started a project that did split the baby for me. Working as a graduate fellow for The Andrew Goodman Foundation, in 2018 I started an initiative within the organization titled Southern Students Vote as a Puffin Democracy Fellow. I aimed to combine the things I knew about the most: working with universities and working in the South.

We set out to continue the work that I did in my undergraduate degree by expanding my research and fieldwork into other states in the region. I hoped to build off of the foundation that I created in Louisiana with youth voting rights. I also wanted to show people that there are college students doing good voting rights work in the South who are unheard of and heretofore unseen.

As college-aged students hold a special place in my heart and in my career, I was and am convinced that the work that they do needs to be quantified and broadcast to the nation. In 2019, we closed out our first year with the project and began to establish Southern Students Vote as a resource hub for college students to learn and develop their own strategies for fighting for voting rights and voter accessibility on their respective campuses. Our network of college students across the region working to hold states accountable, I can't help but think that we are somehow proving to someone that there is good work to be supported.

* * *

What can be gleaned from the cause of getting other young folks to care? Young people are searching for better futures. Particularly when horizons look brighter in a different part of the country, recruiting other young people requires convincing them that the cause is worthy. For the activist seeking to recruit, this specifically means demonstrating to your peers that the long-term gains of progress are worth the short-term disappointments of trying. For Charlie Bonner, a twenty-two-year-old organizer for Progress Texas, the key is to get people to understand that securing your future starts with you.

"People are not our saviors," Charlie insists, because he believes that "we are imperfect people working for a more perfect cause." Charlie speaks from experience. A Virginia native whose Texas roots go back to the original landowners of the state ("old country Texas," as he likes to call it), Charlie's interest in politics started when he was twelve years old when his civics teacher got him involved in the Obama campaign.

He moved to Texas in search for connection to his family's roots, attending the University of Texas in Austin. His undergraduate thesis took him on a cross-county road trip through the continental United States in search for the people's meaning of democracy. Now, as an organizer for progressive causes in one of the most rambunctious state capitals in the South, he believes that the key is to do the work "now," rather than wait on someone else to make the necessary changes, because "we don't have the benefit of being a visionary." Organizers are trying to make change now, and build the dream later.

Such is the cause—sticking around and hoping a few people will care as much as you do, catching people before the disillusionment sets in. In addition to staying, part of the gig is getting other people to stay, too.

When you are younger, you are taught to believe in the ability to work hard and make things happen. Perhaps you witness a groundbreaking event and it causes you to believe that the status quo can be changed, or maybe it's just the naïveté of youth; whatever the cause, young people tend to start off on more optimistic footing than their older counterparts.

Even if a young person is apathetic—though studies show that this is more a generalization than a reality[57]—they are more likely to listen and more likely to be put to work on a cause they believe in. If you wait too long, you may find that your peers have resigned to the fate of a doomed South, and it becomes much harder to recruit.

Back home in Louisiana, Baton Rouge native and a twenty-five-year-old community organizer Helen Frink would likely agree with Charlie on that point, though the power of persuasion cannot be understated when it comes to recruiting organizers on the ground. However, it is important to know and understand your audience. The inability to understand the context in which you are working and to whom you are speaking is a fatal flaw that often inflicts organizers, especially those not raised in the region where they seek to work.

"If you talk at someone about something they either don't understand or don't really care about, they're not gonna be engaged," Helen cautioned.

Helen made waves in 2018 when a local video she starred in went viral, garnering more than 670,000 views from across

---

57 Anja Neundorf and Kaat Smets, "Let the Millenials Grow Up (The Apathetic Youth, and Other Myths)," *Washington Post*, May 19, 2014, https://www.washingtonpost.com/news/monkey-cage/wp/2014/05/19/let-the-millennials-grow-up-the-apathetic-youth-and-other-myths/?noredirect=on.

the world. The video, titled "Why Louisiana Stays Poor,"[58] features Helen holding the state government and big businesses accountable for taking advantage of tax credits while many Louisiana residents fall below the poverty law. Helen was working as a volunteer for Together Baton Rouge, a coalition of community organizations in the Louisiana capital.

When it comes to organizing people, Helen puts it plainly: "It's not a 'them' problem, it's a 'you' problem and how you're presenting [the information]."

It's a you problem. In other words, you the activist make the decision whether to stay and do the work or to leave and never come back. You the activist decides to understand the great significance of recruiting as many people as possible to join your team—and that if you cannot get those people, you might want to look at switching your tactics. While no one should ever switch their values—the fight for equality in human dignity is non-negotiable—anyone working to engage people who they do not know should be willing to adjust their rhetoric to the context.

In Helen's case, this meant demonstrating to people in simple terms the complexity of the Louisiana tax code, and how that tax code worked to the detriment of the state's poor.

---

58   "Why Louisiana Stays Poor," Together Baton Rouge, November 20, 2018, youtube.com/watch?v=sZl2N7YlgNs.

Other contexts may require a serious inquiry into how your audience learns, and what your audience receives, in order to most effectively communicate your values to them.

Dana Sweeney, a twenty-five-year-old organizer in Montgomery, Alabama and one of the most compelling activists for the South that I have ever known, makes a point of convincing his peers to stay dedicated to the region by blatantly acknowledging its flaws while also imploring young Southerners that they are the only ones who can do anything to stop it. His audience receives him so well because he is unapologetic in his values, and relentless in his kindness. I have witnessed him move an audience to tears with his words, and to action with a simple Facebook post. As Dana likes to say, when the horrific events that victimize the South don't inspire you, they should motivate you.

The obligation to stay, and to convince others to stay, is borne from the recognition that with each person lost there is one less foot soldier in the battle to save our region. That is how the obligation manifests: first, the feeling of obligation to stay, and then, the obligation to get others to stay, too. When a problem arises, the young South don't wait on someone to save them.

The sense of obligation, then, is not a self-aggrandizing feeling that *only I can do this*. While in some sense the obligation to stay requires that people feel confident in their ability to make change on their own, it is more complicated than that. We don't say *if not me, then who?* because we believe we are the only person who is capable. We also ask who else is able to take on the task and how we can bring those people to the cause. *If not me, then who?* is not just a feeling, but a call to action.

CHAPTER 7

TAKE IT TO THE ALTAR

Wade in the water
Wade in the water, children
Wade in the water
God's gonna trouble the water.

- NEW JUBILEE SONGS AS SUNG BY

THE FISK JUBILEE SINGERS

While the obligation to serve may be inherent in all Southern activists, the pathway there is not entirely uniform. For many people, the road most commonly traveled toward the obligation to serve is paved by one's service in the pulpit.

Like the humidity on a summer day, religion is an inescapable force in the Deep South.

Specifically, the Protestant Christian faith dominates the region; as anyone who has driven down Interstates ten, twenty, and ninety-five knows, one cannot travel more than several miles on the interstate without passing a megachurch or a mega cross.

According to the Hartford Institute for Religious Research, seven of the ten largest megachurches in the country are located in Alabama, Georgia, North Carolina, South Carolina, and Texas.[59] The largest megachurch in the country is televangelist Joel Osteen's Lakewood Church in Houston, Texas with a weekly congregation of 43,500 people.[60] In total, the South boasts forty-eight point six percent of all mega churches in the country. The importance cannot be understated; as others have noted, "the influence of a dominant evangelical culture [has] shaped the region's social mores, religious minorities . . . cultural forms, charged racial interactions, and political practices."[61]

While the denominations vary—most people know the South for evangelical Baptists, but I grew up around Methodists,

---

59 "Database of Megachurches in the U.S.," Hartford Institute for Religion Research, last accessed October 6, 2019, http://hirr. hartsem.edu/cgi-bin/mega/db.pl?db=default&uid=default&view_ records=1&ID=*&sb=3&so=descend.

60 Ibid.

61 Paul Harvey, "Race, Culture, and Religion in the American South," Oxford Research Encyclopedia of Religion (March 2015), https://oxfordre.com/religion/view/10.1093/ acrefore/9780199340378.001.0001/acrefore-9780199340378-e-7.

Episcopalians, and more—the dominance of the Christian faith in Southern culture is impossible to deny or ignore. Furthermore, a number of religious practices are present throughout the region, including the Jewish, Quaker, and Muslim faiths, among many others.[62] In other words, religion courses through the veins of every Southerner.

For worse, religion has been used to justify slavery and the succession of the Southern states in the Civil War, and the apartheid state under Jim Crow. Religion continues to permeate conversations regarding a woman's right to choose, the human rights of LGBTQ people, and the efficacy of sex education, among other topics.

For better, religion serves as a binding agent for civil rights advocates, including the Civil Rights Movement which ended Jim Crow. To this day, religious leaders doubly serve as moral leaders in the fight for voting rights, civil rights, reproductive justice, and more. In any case, religion is inescapable.

* * *

---

62 Charles Reagan Wilson, "Religion and the U.S. South," Southern Spaces (March 16, 2004), https://southernspaces.org/2004/over-view-religion-and-us-south. "What Is the Truth About American Muslims?" Interfaith Alliance and Religious Freedom Education Project of the First Amendment Center, https://www.tolerance.org/magazine/publications/what-is-the-truth-about-american-muslims.

When you are a child raised in a Southern Christian home, church on Sunday is a set-in-stone weekly meeting with Jesus.

As a kid, you might go to Bible study during the school year and vacation Bible school during the summer. You might have joined your high school's Fellowship of Christian Athletes early in the morning before school to pray before the flag (even if, like me, you were not even an athlete). You might lament the people who have turned their backs on Jesus; your naïveté of life's mistakes leading you to believe that every adverse decision is just another step taken away from the pearly gates. Church was not optional.

If you're sick, then you should take it to the altar.

I can still hear my stepmother's voice as she pried me out of bed each Sunday as I tried for naught to fake ill or otherwise avoid going to church. I was raised in the church, and it molded who I am today. I haven't been to church in nearly a decade, but I still find myself longing for communion every few Sundays or so. Despite my resistance to much of what I was taught, there is no denying what it gave me and many Southern organizers.

Religion is a fuel and a tool; if you don't know how to take it to the altar then you won't reach the souls necessary to make change.

While I shied away from church growing up, today I find it hard to deny the powerful skill of reaching hearts and minds at the pulpit. After all, even I am not immune to the reach of the church. No matter how independent I became, there was no escaping the influence of Sunday morning service—to this day, I can still recite the Apostles Creed on command.

Children become young people who develop their own takes on religion. I decided to keep my faith in Jesus, or at least bits and pieces of it, and carry my spirituality along with me as a motivator for progressive change. I disagreed greatly with the socially conservative lessons I learned, but at the end of the day I still believed in my religion. I did not want to revoke Christianity, but I did not want to endorse what I considered a foul interpretation of Christ's teachings.

I grew to believe that Jesus called us to action, and for me that meant acting with compassion and righteous indignation against all forms of prejudice and injustice. I was inspired by the likes of Martin Luther King, Jr. who in countless sermons invoked Christ's command to his followers to eliminate injustice.

I even got a little rebellious, getting a tattoo of Luke 1:45 on my waist when I was sixteen years old, which remains one of my favorite verses. "You are blessed because you have faith,"

God tells Mary, who is having some understandable doubts about bringing the One True King into this world. If Mary of all people needed reassurance of her calling, I thought, then maybe I'm not in bad shape after all with these college admissions exams. My faith will probably never carry me inside a church, but at least it can anchor me in some personal sense. And, when used properly, religious language compels social justice. Despite my misgivings, I still understand religion as a justification to fight tirelessly for common human dignity.

I am not alone.

* * *

Young people across the South not only contend with their religion, but leverage their connection to their faith to activate their communities. No matter where they currently stand, young people who grew up in the church understand that they cannot simply leave it behind. The pull is just too strong, and many of the people who are still there need our help. We may not agree with them all the time, but the church is our people.

It is no wonder, then, that young people credit their own inspirations as being partly religious—begrudgingly or otherwise. Dana Sweeney, twenty-five, credits his Catholic upbringing as having inspired him to go into social justice work. While he is no longer a weekly mass goer, he feels grateful for what

Catholicism gave him. Dana is an organizer for the Alabama Appleseed Center for Law and Justice, working primarily on the issue of predatory payday lending in the state. He also serves as a Puffin Democracy Fellow for The Andrew Goodman Foundation, in which capacity he works with the Alabama Rights Restoration Project to help inform people with felony convictions of their right to vote. Dana spends a lot of time working with disenfranchised communities, and credits his Catholic upbringing as a primary driver for his dedication to social justice work.

"I think I'm really grateful for what Catholicism gifted to me growing up," Dana says, explaining the tenants of the Catholic faith, including the orientation toward justice and the idea that grace can be found in anyone.

However, what the church giveth, it also taketh away. "I'm not welcome in the Catholic Church [because I am queer]. Nonetheless, it was one of the most formative components of my upbringing and remains one of the driving influences in the work that I do," Dana remarks. "So holding that contradiction is something that I think about a lot, you know."

In early high school Dana felt that contradiction viscerally. An otherwise normal day at mass, a visiting priest gave a homily against LGBTQ people, or as Dana recalls, "how the homosexuals are trying to take over America and kill God." In what he considers an act of political protest, Dana got so upset and angry that he refused to take communion, despite upsetting his parents. "Afterwards, [my dad] was like, 'why didn't you get up to take communion?' And I was like, because that was not God. That was not and I will not toast to this. I will not take this as the word or the body of Christ. I just cannot accept that."

Like many young folks, Dana accepted the form of Christianity that he saw most just: one that accepts all at the altar. The core tenant of the Catholic faith that he identifies with, that divinity resides within each person, is clearly reflected in the work that he does. Working at the Appleseed Center, Dana has advocated against predatory payday lending policies which hit the poorest people in one of the poorest states in the nation. He began his young career in service, working as an ambassador for The Andrew Goodman Foundation at the University of Alabama advocating for students to be able to vote absentee on campus.

"I think the other core pillar of Catholicism that drives me is that idea that we are 'saved by works' rather than 'saved by faith alone,' which is to say that my actions in relation to others are what matter and what might make any route to God," Dana concludes. "The only way to access the divine is through service and community with others, through acts of mending the world and combating injustice right where you are. It's a propulsive faith. It's a conviction that nothing holy comes without getting your hands dirty."

His faith, like that of countless other young people who decide to take on the problems of our region, reflect that of his predecessors: a faith rooted in radical service. That evergreen contradiction, between genuine gratitude and genuine indignation, of not belonging and refusing to accept things as they are, is the driving force behind social reform. You cannot run away from your faith, but you cannot let it be your downfall, either.

Next door in Georgia, Joey Wozniak, twenty-six, believes that religion is both one of the most important outlets to reaching out to people and one of the most misunderstood aspects of the South. Joey works in philanthropy, as a managing partner of Mile 22 Associates, and spends a lot of time thinking about why the impact of the philanthropy movement does not exist in the Southeast. "There's a hell of a lot of preconceived notions about Christianity," Joey explains to me. As he sees it, religion is the "main civic platform that people use to meet [others in their community]."

"I classify church as a civic organization with religious beliefs. To discredit their impact on their community through other types of service, that's not fair whatsoever. And for many folks too, it's their only connection to the outside world," Joey continues. "People that attend their church are teachers at other schools or professors at the local community college, or the one person with financial means. And that [church community is] where you can learn about different colleges, or make connections to getting an internship or job or whatever else. And it's [the church community's] lifeblood, and I think [people] underestimate that a fair amount."

Joey isn't wrong. Many young Southerners identify with religion as a tool for community building. In my experience, it is common to not believe in church but to still rely on church leaders to rally religious communities in volunteer and service efforts. Churches are still reliable sources of community service, and will often remain the last stronghold in an economically underserved area.

The common connection of the Christian faith binds together the African American community, in particular. Black churches functioned as the satellite offices of civil rights leaders, and to this day function as a main source of moral clarity for Black church goers seeking out answers for today's problems. Black churches are targets of white supremacy—from the Sixteenth Street Baptist Church bombing in 1963 Birmingham to the Emanuel African Methodist Episcopal Church massacre in 2015 Charleston, South Carolina—and targets of politicians who seek out endorsements from pastors of historically Black churches. I personally may never go to church again, but I will never disparage my Black church family and what they instilled in me, either.

* * *

In places like middle Alabama where Dana works, the connection to faith and social justice requires understanding the vast influence of religion in everyday life. In 2017, *U.S. News* ranked Alabama as tied with Mississippi as the most religious state in the country; a whopping eighty-six percent of Alabama adults identified as Christian.[63]

Accordingly, evangelical voters dominate daily life; according to *Pew*, fifty-percent of Alabama adults go to church at least once per week, seventy-three percent pray every day, and fifty percent cite the Bible as a source of guidance for right and wrong.[64] Political representation also correlates strongly with religious affiliation; according to *CNN*, almost all of the Alabama senators who recently voted to pass an almost-absolute abortion ban in early 2019 cited their Christian faith in their biographies.[65]

Hearkening back to Jim Crow, the KKK famously used religion as justification for its terror and political power grabs

---

63 Gaby Galvin, Most Religious States in America, *U.S. News*, August 22, 2017, https://www.usnews.com/news/best-states/slideshows/10-most-religious-states-in-america?slide=11.

64 Adults in Alabama: Religious Composition of Adults in Alabama, Pew Forum, last accessed October 6, 2019, https://www.pewforum.org/religious-landscape-study/state/alabama/.

65 Daniel Burke, "Yes, Abortion Activists Use Religious Language. It's Still About Politics," *CNN*, May 23, 2019, https://www.cnn.com/2019/05/23/politics/abortion-religion-views-alabama/index.html/.

across the South—one of their most significant political feats was helping elect Bull Connor, the Birmingham Commissioner of Public Safety and infamous white supremacist and segregationist, during the Civil Rights Movement.[66]

On the other hand, recent focus has turned on the electoral influence of Black evangelical voters, as the voting bloc helped Alabama's first Democratic US Senator in more than twenty years. Many religious leaders in Alabama fought unsuccessfully to stop the anti-abortion efforts in the state, including at least one lawmaker who identifies as pro-choice and Christian.[67]

In other words, to change lives in a place like middle Alabama, you're going to have to meet them where they are: the pulpit.

As equally important as acknowledging the power of religion is acknowledging that religion is not simply held by the religious right. To be sure, religious conservatives have taken over the popular perception of Southern spirituality. For the last several decades, religious progressives have been drowned out by the cacophony that is the religious right. A

66 "Ku Klux Klan: A History of Racism," Southern Poverty Law Center, March 1, 2011, https://www.splcenter.org/20110228/ku-klux-klan-history-racism.

67 Meagan Flynn, "'A typical male answer': Only 3 Women Had a Voice in Alabama Senate As 25 Men Passed Abortion Ban," *Washington Post*, May 15, 2019 https://beta.washingtonpost.com/nation/2019/05/15/typical-male-answer-only-women-had-voice-alabama-senate-men-passed-abortion-ban/.

potent combination of political will and years of fomenting a presence in the media, schools, and other spaces in public life has all but cemented the religious right's dominance in the popular conscious.

If you let this narrative fool you, you might forget that Martin Luther King was a reverend.

Progressive religion is a lifeblood of the larger progressive movement in the region. The Poor People's Campaign is proof positive of the spiritual blood that courses through the veins of the movement to progress the South. The Poor People's Campaign was first initiated by Martin Luther King, Jr. and the Southern Christian Leadership Conference, who wanted to engage in "a fight by capable, hard workers against dehumanization, discrimination, and poverty wages in the richest country in the world."[68] Fifty years later, activists revived the movement to address contemporary issues of social justice— including environmental justice, voting rights, and other issues disproportionately impacting poor people in this country.[69] Reverend William Barber, a founder of the Poor People's Campaign and former president of the NAACP of North Carolina, often remarks on the spiritual imperative to serve.

---

68 "Dr. King's Vision: The Poor People's Campaign of 1967-68," Poor People's Campaign, last accessed October 6, 2019, https://www. poorpeoplescampaign.org/history/.

69 Ibid.

The future of the region turns on changing hearts and minds. In the South, those hearts and minds are molded in the church.

* * *

No matter one's individual belief, there is no denying religion's hold on the South. Rather than deny religion, however, we can work to use religion as a bridge between change-makers and the community.

This doesn't require conforming to the faith; many community leaders who work with churches are not religious themselves. This also does not require compromising who you are to talk to people who may deny your identity on religious grounds; like Dana so demonstrates, you don't have to stand for hateful rhetoric to still find value in the church as a community.

Instead, consider reframing the church as a potential place to reach hearts and minds, rather than a breeding ground for oppressive hate. The Christian church has a complicated history, strife with stories of oppression and redemption. Like it or not, communities rely on churches. Rather than turning away from that, we need to find ways to bring our message to the altar.

If faith without works is dead, then the young people working on the ground are keeping spirituality alive in their own way.

The reconciliation with religion is simply a part of the larger reckoning that Southern activists do every day, as they work in a region that rejects their dedication to it.

They understand that changing hearts and minds is going to require a little faith, so to speak.

CHAPTER 8

THE FUNDAMENTAL CONTRADICTION

Fellow-citizens, pardon me, allow me to ask, why am I called upon to speak here to-day? What have I, or those I represent, to do with your national independence? Are the great principles of political freedom and of natural justice, embodied in that Declaration of Independence, extended to us?

- FREDERICK DOUGLASS, WHAT TO THE
SLAVE IS THE FOURTH OF JULY?

There is an inherent contradiction in deciding to stay and do the necessary work of progress in a region where progress is halted every step of the way.

Legal philosopher Duncan Kennedy used the term "funda-mental contradiction" to describe American society. In his words, "the goal of individual freedom is both dependent on and incompatible with the communal coercive action that is necessary to achieve it."[70]

I think that is a pretty apt description of the condition that inflicts the young Southern activist. At once, we seek indi-vidual gratification and a sense of belonging, which is both dependent on and incompatible with the obligation to work on the progressive cause back home.

Stated simply, if you decide to stay, you will spend your time justifying your decision to love the place that rejects your point of view (read: existence).

For me, this manifested in playing the Devil's advocate. This often came off as disrespectfully questioning my elders (*That doesn't make sense. If the Lord says we love every one, how come we hate those people?*), or an outright rejection of the stated premise (*That doesn't make sense. If we are afraid that criminals will not be affected by gun laws because criminals don't care about laws, then why do we have laws in the first place?*). In other words, I was an obnoxious child, but such

70 Duncan Kennedy, The Structure of Blackstone's Commentaries, 28 Buff. L. Rev. 205, 211-214 (1979). Available at: https://digitalcom-mons.law.buffalo.edu/buffalolawreview/vol28/iss2/2.

is the case of one slowly being inflicted with the fundamental contradiction.

The condition spreads slowly.

If you live in tough conditions, you might find yourself attributing your family's struggles to the futility of the place where you live, and start seeking ways out. You might first tell yourself that you are just moving to another part of town where the kids look happier and richer. Then, as you start to get older, you might start to dream bigger and seek to move to another part of the state or the country, where it seems like there are more opportunities. At this point, the guilt sets in, because you feel like you have left your people behind as you start to see your own success.

You have then reached the crossroads from which the fundamental contradiction can be cured or you can decide to live with your condition: you stay or you go.

I cured myself of the fundamental contradiction the moment I decided to leave Louisiana to pursue educational opportunities outside of the state. I took the red pill and left.

The young people who stayed, however, still feel the condition coursing through their veins. Every day, they actively choose to buck the easy way out, and live with the fact that they are working to change a place that actively opposes their existence.

Particularly if you are marginalized, the fundamental contradiction commands a recognition that you may fail to achieve your goals if you stay—both individual gratification and community redemption—but you cannot hope to achieve your goals without staying. Understanding that there are only two cures to the disease—change your views or leave—the young people who live and work in the South every day decide to simply live with their condition.

* * *

All is not lost in succumbing to the fundamental contradiction, as those who do can also use their position to their advantage. If an element of the condition is the understanding that you cannot untie yourself from your community, then it stands to reason that those afflicted have a unique understanding of their communities.

After all, to know what you're choosing means to know what you are not choosing. If you know why you are not choosing to change your views, then your understanding of those opposing views puts you in a position to leverage that understanding to meet your ends. Those who get their fundamental contradiction know thine enemy.

To make actual change in the South often requires making strange bedfellows, and to embrace your fundamental contradiction effectively is to know how to work with unlikely allies to reach an end. The movement for social justice is a constant lesson in compromise, which is often unfair and painful, but concurrently necessary.

Passing the Civil Rights Act of 1964 required working with Lyndon B. Johnson, who reportedly referred to the legislation as "the nigger bill."[71] Martin Luther King would work closely with President Johnson, who signed the bill into law in 1964. More recently, progressive activists in Louisiana worked with the conservative and Koch brothers-funded Americans for Prosperity to successfully pass a constitutional amendment to abolish non-unanimous juries in the state.[72] The law was a remnant of Jim Crow-era policies which created countless false or overbroad convictions and rose the state to among the most heavily incarcerated places on Earth.

In each case, radical progress required a radical comprise of one's wholly justified inclination to reject keeping company with the ones who would otherwise seek your oppression.

---

71   Adam Serwer, "Lyndon Johnson Was a Civil Rights Hero. But Also A Racist." *MSNBC*, April 11, 2014, http://www.msnbc.com/msnbc/lyndon-johnson-civil-rights-racism.

72   "Koch Group Backs Louisiana Move Toward Unanimous Juries," *Associated Press*, October 1, 2018, https://www.nola.com/politics/2018/10/koch_louisiana_unanimous_jurie.html.

The progressive change maker makes the completely contra-dictory choice to decide that in this case, keeping company is just more prudent.

While this does not require the concurrent rejection of one's values—indeed, both of these examples are storied with progressives very explicit in noting that just because we are friends now doesn't mean we won't still be enemies tomorrow—the inevitability of being a Southern progressive is learning to fight in learning to compromise.

The most successful young activists in the South understand the fundamental contradiction intuitively, even if they can-not express it in explicit terms.

In my own observation, young people tend to know that they are going to have to make some hard choices about the peo-ple with whom they deal. Arekia Bennet, the twenty-six-year-old organizer and the Executive Director of Mississippi Votes, acknowledged that her organizing background in Mississippi has left her with a "radical history of organizing young people."

"I think one of the ways that I've been able to get around that is like, really good relationships on both sides of the fence," Are-kia said. "[For example,] I've done some advocacy work around women's pay equity. And one of the pieces of legislation that we were trying to push last year was a bipartisan issue. And so I still have folks who . . . trust and believe in me enough to [know] my ability to move people [toward an issue]."

In my own experience, working with unexpected allies comes easiest to young people, because the young are not yet tainted by the realities of political cynicism. Instead, as young people, we are so motivated by our cause that we are willing to do anything, and talk to anyone, to progress that cause.

This strategy has worked for Arekia. During her tenure at Mississippi Votes, the organization has registered thousands of Mississippi residents to vote; the *New York Times* reported that from August to September 2018 alone, the organization registered 2,000 voters ahead of the midterm elections.

The organization has a reputation for being nonpartisan, while its mission remains "stay vocal, act local." As Arekia explained to the *New York Times*, "We want to engage and empower people so that they see themselves not just as a number but as a viable character in their own lives. This is about self-determination."[73]

* * *

---

73   Audra D.S. Burch, "A New Class of Voting Rights Activists Picks Up the Mantle in Mississippi," *New York Times*, September 25, 2018, https://www.nytimes.com/2018/09/25/us/freedom-summer-mississippi-votes.html.

The fundamental contradiction also implies a certain strategy in building a broader coalition.

This strategy involves knowing that broad movements require a broad coalition. Megan Newsome, now a twenty-three-year-old graduate student at the University of California in Santa Barbara, was a student ambassador for The Andrew Goodman Foundation at the University of Florida as an undergraduate student. A Florida native, she was interested early on in increasing the political power of her peers in a state that holds incredible importance in the national electorate.

As a result, she spent her time registering young voters at the University of Florida and helping students stay informed about upcoming elections—an astrophysics major, Megan was particularly interested in engaging STEM students who don't normally participate in the political process. Her own research, and the findings of the National Study of Learning, Voting, and Engagement, indicate that STEM majors are among the lowest turnout bloc of young voters.[74]

Ever the inquirer, Megan discovered that students before her tried unsuccessfully to get an early voting polling location on

---

74 See Nancy Thomas et al, "Democracy Counts: A Report on U.S. College and University Voting 2012-2016," Institute for Democracy & Higher Education, Tufts University's Jonathan M. Tisch College of Civic Life (2017), https://idhe.tufts.edu/sites/default/files/NSLVE%20Report%202012-2016-092117%5B3%5D.pdf.

UF's campus. So, in spring 2015, a young Megan and a team of students picked up the baton, meeting with local elections supervisors and state legislators to request an early voting polling location at the student union at the University of Florida, so that students can more easily access early voting.

They were immediately met with resistance, so they tried drafting legislation and working with state lawmakers. After that too was unsuccessful, the students found an unlikely ally: the federal courts in Florida and the US Constitution. In 2018, Megan and a group of other students, along with the League of Women Voters of Florida and The Andrew Goodman Foundation, sued the state of Florida.

"For three straight years everything I was doing was failing," Megan said. So when she was asked to be a plaintiff in the lawsuit, she was ready to fight. Still, she had reservations. "[The League of Women Voters asked], so do you want to be a plaintiff? And that's a tough question. I don't know if it's every day when you get asked to be a plaintiff in a lawsuit. So I did have to, like, think through that and make sure I was ready to be involved in the legal battle."

The students alleged that the state's refusal to put a polling place on campus violated the twenty-sixth Amendment of the Constitution because their actions discriminated against college students. The students won a preliminary injunction from a Florida federal court, which forced the state's hand and required them to place a polling location at the University of Florida.[75]

Students across the state saw the results of Megan's work and followed suit in their own advocacy by petitioning to their county boards of elections to get early voting locations on their own respective campuses. By November 2018, students not only at the University of Florida voted early on campus, but new early voting locations popped up at colleges across Florida as the lawsuit created momentum for other students to request polling places on their own campuses. Third times the charm, and only possible with a broad coalition.

* * *

If you are marginalized, you additionally have to spend your time defending (to yourself and to others) the place you call home even if that place does not seem to have your back. This means living with the fundamental contradiction within yourself, but also the criticism from others who don't understand why you choose to live in a place that might literally deny your existence.

---

75 Steve Bousquet, "Judge: Florida's early voting-on-campus ban shows 'stark pattern of discrimination,'" *Tampa Bay Times*, July 24, 2018, https://www.tampabay.com/florida-politics/ buzz/2018/07/24/judge-faults-state-and-approves-early-voting-on- college-university-campuses/.

Even though I cured myself of the fundamental contradiction, I still face constant questioning from those who don't understand why a Black woman would want to go back to the South. Why do I defend a place that is denying my right to choose at the same time? Why would I want to live in a place that allows Black women like me to face higher rates of maternal mortality, higher rates of domestic violence, and higher rates of poverty? Why would I ever want to interact with the same people from whom I have heard the "N" word?

These are reasonable questions, but honestly, the people who ask them just don't get it.

Those of us who defend the South know that we are not defending the oppressive state where we were raised. We defend the people who suffer, and the culture that suffers as a result. Importantly, we defend the potential to make it a better place.

"My home does not reflect my values," Charlie Bonner, the twenty-three-year-old organizer for MOVE Texas, said. Charlie, who spends most of his time in the Texas legislature defending the rights of people of color, women, and LGBTQ people, was not explaining why he left. He was explaining why he does the work: because his home does not reflect his values, he is compelled to stay and change that. "I want to turn Texas blue very desperately."

On the other hand, Helen Frink, the twenty-five-year-old community organizer from Baton Rouge, Louisiana wants to dispel the notion that this contradiction, and the obligation it imposes, isn't necessarily a bad thing. As a white woman from a middle class background, Helen knows that she could move to a more progressive place. She also knows, however, the privilege she can leverage, so she chose to embrace the contradiction.

"I'm not *stuck* stuck here, and a lot of people are *stuck* stuck here, so I want to use that power for good," she explained. A key factor in this contradiction is knowing that your voice may not be welcomed. But the toll of living with the fundamental contradiction pales in comparison to being in a position to raise that voice on behalf of others. "Yes, I [feel] obligated [to stay]," Helen said. "But not . . . in debt and not in a negative way."

You are not in debt because this place doesn't owe you anything. But, this contradiction is not negative because the very nature of staying to do the work, despite the risk of negative feedback, is inherently a positive thing. After all, the work you do as a young organizer is largely on-the-ground, working with the people for whom negative social and governmental policy affect. We are working to protect the most vulnerable, not the powers that be, and those voices that matter the most.

Still, grappling with that contradiction means understanding that the only way out is by leaving home. And with that understanding comes the temptation to take the out. Whether you have cured yourself of the fundamental contradiction or decided to live with it, the residual guilt is nevertheless inescapable. For me, even as someone who plans to come back home and whose career focuses primarily in the Southern region, I constantly suffer from the nagging feeling that I decided to take the out when I left Louisiana. For the ones who never left, they may constantly feel a nagging feeling that they could have left and chose to stay in the turmoil. Alas, a contradiction within a contradiction.

"People are like, you've never tried to leave, [but] that's not true. I literally have tried to leave and Mississippi has drug me back," Arekia Bennett told me. "Every time I have tried to leave there is something that has literally called my name."

For Arekia, even moving next door to Birmingham, Alabama after college for a stint did not fare well for her. The pull was too strong, as she felt compelled to fill the void for missing voices in the fight for human rights. Dana Sweeney had a similar feeling. A Truman scholar from Georgia who graduated from the University of Alabama, Dana had the opportunity to travel and work in different places across the country. It didn't suit him well. "It was a paradox . . . I know where home is for me and I in many ways am not welcomed or wanted," Dana said. "And rather than just cede that, that really agitated me to stick around and reclaim where I am from."

A paradox, indeed. There is no better time to consider relocating than when you are young, post-high school or post-college, and feeling like your voice just isn't being heard (and, I'd add, what better reason to leave?).

But you also feel like you are the only person who can reach out—you are from there, you know your people, so who else can speak to the disenfranchised without being condescending, and the powers on high without being dismissed? Sure, you won't be successful all the time (or even half the time), and your ideas will be mocked, and you will be told to just move on.

But, you will have other moments: Dana, whose work helps people with felony convictions register to vote in Alabama; Arekia, who activates Mississippi's youth population in the thousands; Helen, who called out to the world (literally, she's on YouTube) the inner workings of a tax policy that harms Louisiana's poor; and Charlie, who fights for civil rights every day in the Texas legislature.

Those moments remind us that this fundamental contradiction—to stay in a place where you may not be welcomed—is the fuel that drives young people across the South to work, without whom the future of the region would be increasingly uncertain.

CHAPTER 9

WHY ARE WE HERE?

———

How curious a land is this,—how full of untold story, of tragedy and laughter, and the rich legacy of human life; shadowed with a tragic past, and big with future promise!

- WILLIAM EDWARD BURGHARDT DU BOIS, "OF THE
BLACK BELT," FROM THE SOULS OF BLACK FOLK

In summer 2019, the nation watched Alabama pass a total ban on abortion, the sort of legislation meant to challenge the Supreme Court's precedent in *Roe v. Wade.*

Then came a wave of similar legislation in Mississippi, then Louisiana; shortly before Alabama, Georgia passed its own six-week abortion ban. Anti-choice activists launched a full-on assault on women.

While hindsight is twenty-twenty, it is clear that we all saw it coming. The 2016 election of Donald Trump, who promised a war on choice, and the subsequent appointment of expressly anti-choice judges and Supreme Court justices, clearly foretold an attack on women's rights.[76] With state legislatures in the region overwhelmingly dominated by anti-choice legislators, the region was once again left flatfooted by the sudden rush of oppressive legislation (it was never actually sudden).

While the nation looked down upon the backwards South, I observed Helmi Henkin.

Helmi Henkin is in her early twenties and a 2018 graduate of the University of Alabama. She also serves as the Chair of the West Alabama Clinic Defenders, and the Treasurer of the Yellowhammer Fund, an abortion fund for women in Alabama.[77] In her role, Helmi is on the frontlines of the Alabama war against women, coordinating and training clinic escorts so that women who sought abortions could do so safely and anonymously.

I encountered Helmi's work on Facebook; a noted friend of this book, Dana Sweeney, posted about a fundraiser that she

---

76 For example, see Elie Mystal, "Donald Trump and the Plot to Take Over the Courts," *The Nation*, July 15, 2019, https://www.thenation.com/article/trump-mcconnel-court-judges-plot/.

77 The Yellowhammer Fund, last accessed October 6, 2019, https://yellowhammerfund.org/.

organized for her work in the wake of Alabama passing its crippling abortion law. From my comfortable position (I had no immediate concerns about my right to choose while sitting in Washington, DC), I observed intently as Helmi did the work in the midst of a storm. She continued to do her job in a state that threatened criminal penalties for doctors performing abortions and demonstrated an outright hostility to women at the state level.

The rest of the nation derided the backwards Alabamans (how could they, after all, vote for state legislators who would take their rights away?), and people like me looked at the state in shame while sitting comfortably in a place that will never deny me my rights as a woman.

Meanwhile, Helmi continued to do her job.

Five decades earlier, a group of college students decided to confront the evil facing them head on, this time at a lunch table instead of a clinic parking lot. During the Civil Rights Movement, coordinated campaigns to desegregate public spaces spread through the South. As the *New York Times* recounts, students at North Carolina Agricultural and Technical College—eighteen-year-old Ezell Blair, Jr.; nineteen-year-old Franklin McCain.; seventeen-year-old Joseph McNeil; and eighteen-year-old David Richmond—staged sit-ins at several restaurants to protest segregation during the Civil Rights Movement.[78]

Known as the Greensboro Four, over the course of a weekend they attracted hundreds more protesters. By summer 1960, these sit-ins had spread across fifty cities across the South, paving the way for desegregation at lunch counters. Their actions led to the formation of the Student Nonviolent Coordinating Committee, perhaps best known for its actions under now-Representative John Lewis's leadership.

* * *

Arguably the most significant barrier to progressive success in the region is the apathy developed over time. This is, in part, a result of the narrative machine which presents the South as a foregone conclusion, and consistently looks down on the failure the region outputs while ignoring its potential.

A sentiment internalized by insiders and projected down by outsiders, much of the South cannot seem to dig itself out of the notion that resistance is futile. Notwithstanding the barriers we face by the oppressors who actively work to

---

78   Maggie Astor, "7 Times in History When Students Turned to Activism," *New York Times*, https://www.nytimes.com/2018/03/05/us/student-protest-movements.html."45 Students Seized in Greensboro Sit-In," *New York Times*, April 22, 1960.

foreclose the possibility of hope, we remain in the same spot because no one has faith that we can get ourselves out of it, including ourselves.

We are truly missing the point; while we turn our focus on the state legislatures of the region, we miss out on the opportunity to support the Helmi's. We are here, in this rut, in part because we cannot seem to shift the narrative.

The narrative crowding the popular conscious overshadows these stories and is the primary cause of our inability to succeed in progressive movements. The narrative that prevails is one of a South that is never meant to change. Young folks in the South face particular challenges with perception, which does not give the region the benefit of the doubt and insists that resistance to the status quo is futile.

This narrative is unproductive, as the notion that the South is a foregone conclusion undermines any efforts by young people to convince their peers to join them in making the region better. The narrative stymies the change sought by the activists doing the work every day, because the notion that the South will not change makes these young people look either crazy, naïve, or overly optimistic by those who perpetuate the idea.

Young people who have the opportunity may leave, and young people who don't have the opportunity must stay. In any case, no one wants or should want to be there any longer than they have to unless they are just as backwards as the region they occupy, according to the common refrain.

These narratives do not primarily hurt those who perpetuate them. Instead, they hurt the people who are unrepresented in the narrative, namely, the poor, the person of color, and the otherwise marginalized and disenfranchised. In the region with the largest Black population in the country, these stereotypes insult not only the progress made, but the progress sought.

The detriments do not end with the threshold opportunity gap looming over the region. This notion is seriously racialized and class-based.

One *New York Times* article, titled "Abortion and The Future of the New South," exemplifies how the narrative is a disservice to the disadvantaged.[79] Perhaps more insidiously, the idea is but a passing talking point for the privileged. The premise of the article—that the sweep of abortion laws passed by conservative legislatures in the South threatens to undermine "a set of aspirations of some Southern elites who hoped to rebuild a backward and devastated place into

---

79 Ginia Bellafante, "Abortion and The Future of the New South," *New York Times*, May 16, 2019, https://www.nytimes.com/2019/05/16/nyregion/abortion-millennials-south.html.

a world better aligned with Northern urban values"— misses the same point missed by the overall sentiment of those putting forth a tale of a South meant to fail.

Besides sorely lacking insight into the actual goals of those seeking progress of the South, this idea neglects to realize both the perils of those disenfranchised in the South and the failings of an imperfect North. The goal of progress is not to somehow convert New Orleans to New York City, or Atlanta to Washington, DC. The goal for many is to bring the values which Southerners treasure most—values which include hospitality and spirituality but also a rich culture— into the Twenty-first Century, and make the region a place where all feel welcome at home. The goal is to close the social and economic gap that so plagues our region, by reckoning with our past to move forward.

Moreover, the Northeastern United States may not have a history within the Confederacy, but not all of its history is something to aspire; the region boasts some of the most blatant racial housing and economic segregation in the nation.[80] No one's noses are clean, and even much of the progressive South would prefer to keep the better parts of our culture intact.

---

80 For examples of cities across the country see, Richard Rothstein, *The Color of Law: A Forgotten History of How Our Government Segregated America* (New York: Liveright Publishing, 2017).

Additionally, this narrative of a broken, backwards South that cannot be changed ignores the people who have made changes. These narratives seem to ignore Mariah Parker, for example, the twenty-seven-year-old rapper, PhD student, and city commissioner in Athens, Georgia who was sworn into office holding *The Autobiography of Malcom X* and whose mission is to lift up the hidden problems of the seemingly scenic college town's poor.[81] These narratives ignore Park Cannon, the state representative for Georgia's fifty-eighth district sworn in at twenty-four years old in 2016 and leading the charge for reproductive and LGBTQ rights in the state house.[82]

As one Twitter commentator stated, "You all really need to stop viewing the South as an overwhelmingly racist and white region and start viewing it as vast communities of color and leftist organizations being held hostage by right-wing state governments."[83] Overall, these narratives miss the forest for the trees; instead of looking at the broad landscape of leaders standing their ground at all levels of government, the story told insists on recounting the tired tropes that feed into the popular

---

81 Austyn Gaffney, "From Rap Battles to City Hall—Mariah Parker Sets the Stage for Young Political Leaders," *Scalawag*, April 1, 2019, https://www.scalawagmagazine.org/2019/04/mariah-parker-feature/.

82 Leila Ettachfini, "This Queer, Black Georgia Lawmaker Refuses to Be Called a 'Politician'," *VICE*, May 25, 2018, https://www.vice.com/en_us/article/pava9z/park-cannon-georgia-house.

83 @ReadAndAct_, Twitter, July 22, 2019, https://twitter.com/ReadAndAct_/status/1153369033909121024.

notion of a backwards South. As a result, the arduous battles that women like Mariah Parker, Park Cannon, and countless others wage against the massive political machines that seek to halt progress tends to be relegated only to the active listeners; no popular storytelling appreciates the yeoman's effort put forth by activists and activist politicians on the ground.

* * *

This perception of the backward South permeates throughout the media and undermines the progress being made by playing right into the hands of the dominating class, who maintain power in the region in large part because of the apathy that they work to maintain.

As North Carolina-based journalist Kristin Rawls notes, the media's tropes regard the South as largely rural and uneducated. These stereotypes cut both ways, as "[t]he Right romanticizes us as the 'real America' while the Left treats us a punchline."[84] When national elections roll around, neither the political left nor the political right bother to come down South; we are deemed an electoral inevitability. This creates a self-fulfilling prophecy, whereby the winners and losers are predetermined.

---

84 Kristin Rawls, "The Media's Southern Stereotypes," *The Nation*, April 4, 2012, https://www.salon.com/2012/04/04/the_medias_southern_stereotypes/.

It is no wonder why in 2014, Republicans entrenched total control of statewide offices in the Deep South, until Louisiana Governor John Bel Edwards won just a year later in 2015 and remained the only statewide-elected Democrat until 2017.[85] The popular notion that things can't or won't change results in low political participation on the part of citizens and decreased accountability on the part of politicians.

Mass change comes in the South, then, at a tipping point, when folks' collective horror calls them to action— politicians like Senator Doug Jones from Alabama are elected because his opponent is an alleged child predator, and coastal erosion efforts are granted an imperative in Louisiana when massive floodings in South Louisiana and Texas destroy thousands of lives and homes. There is no new political calculation when the sum of the calculus is already assumed. Those most affected by political failings have to rely on statistical anomalies for progress to occur.

Louisiana native and student activist Zöe Williamson related three insights to me about how this narrative manifest in the context of political participation among young people, namely first-time voters in college. The first take is a product

---

85 Nate Cohn, "Demise of the Southern Democrat is Nearly Complete," *New York Times*, November 5, 2014, https://www.nytimes.com/2014/12/05/upshot/demise-of-the-southern-democrat-is-now-nearly-compete.html.

of age. As she notes, "[I]t's hard for students to care whenever they're focused on their schooling . . . it's a new environment for them and their life is changing dramatically. So they're . . . inwards and not outwards."

Next, she found that because college students live away from their parents, a lack of options for students to vote and register to vote creates an additional barrier to participation. However, the third factor she found is a product of the backwards South stereotype, which results in a systemic lack of resources and knowledge on the part of young people: "There's no one guiding them," she pointed out. "There's no one showing them" the correct way to participate in the political process, and "whenever it is your first time voting, it's scary because you don't have all the information and so for a lot of people that fear . . . overcomes them and they just choose not to vote.

"And once they make that decision the first time, that's pretty much it for them . . . they're probably not ever going to."

* * *

As it is often said, if you tell someone the same lie enough times, soon enough you will start to believe it yourself. As the backwards South narrative persists, eventually young, hopeful Southerners start believing in our region's futility. So, how do we move forward?

Speaking to the *New York Times*, twenty-five-year-old Mississippi Votes Executive Director Arekia Bennett remarked that, "There is a power that transcends our ages." We cannot continue to let these stereotypes become self-fulfilling prophecies. Instead of letting these narratives defeat the progress sought in the South, young activists should take note of their peers who are refusing to believe the hype.

Moving forward additionally requires understanding the people who were raised in the South, who plan to stay in the South, and who are steadfast in their determination to change the South. As Mariah Parker, the Athens City commissioner, said to *The Bitter Southerner*, "People need you. You promised them you would fix these things. You can't go anywhere."[86]

To be fair, there are undoubtedly outlets seeking to provide a platform for the vision of the progressive South. Magazines such as *The Bitter Southerner* and *Scalawag* are but a few examples of places of refuge for criticism and appreciation, as well as narrative-challenging, of the South as a place that we Southerners both love and hate. The Institute for Southern Studies, a research institute founded in the 1970s by civil

---

86 Alison Miller, "Power to the People, No Delay," *Bitter Southerner,* last accessed October 7, 2019, https://bittersoutherner. com/fighting-the-power-in-a-southern-college-town-mariah- parker-linqua-franqa.

rights organizers and based in North Carolina, states as its mission that it seeks to "[draw] attention to the national importance of the South and [offer] an exciting vision of the region—a place brimming with a capacity for progressive change that challenges its reputation as a monolithic, conservative stronghold."[87] Moreover, the region is budding with writers and artists seeking to challenge the common notion of a broken, backwards South.

When young people decide that things need a change, a change happens. That change will continue to be slowed, however, by the pervasive and blatantly untrue tale that there is no work that can be successfully done in the South.

The same people who call for change lament that perhaps change can never happen, such that the people who are working on the ground lose the ability to convince others, and sometimes themselves, that change is possible. The stories untold could show the nation that there are people and causes worth investing into within the region.

There is a story to be told about the young people in the South who decide to confront the challenges the region faces head on, who decide to buck conventional wisdom telling them to get the hell out of dodge while they are still young. Time is

---

87   "History," Institute for Southern Studies, last accessed October 6, 2019, https://www.southernstudies.org/history.

not purely linear; the lessons learned and the passion embedded in the past are not gone. The tactics and the stereotypes we see today are not new, they are recycled material from a past we continue to see manifest in the present. We can learn from them, and we can overcome them.

FACING MY OWN CONTRADICTIONS

———

I laugh so hard I almost choke,
When I think about myself.

— MAYA ANGELOU

When I was a kid I hated sweet iced tea.

I literally spat it out if it was given to me. I hated the taste and the smell; it felt bitter against my tongue. Seriously, I would make a big fuss about it. If anyone dared hand me a glass, I would cross my hands and refuse. At some point, I stopped remembering what iced tea actually tasted like because I hadn't tried it in years, but I just knew for a fact that I hated iced tea anyway. *Everyone* loved sweet iced tea—I thought it wasn't worth the hype.

You're not from here, Valencia, if you don't drink sweet tea! my friends would tease. That sounded good to me—I hated this place and I hated its sweet iced tea, too.

Fine, then I'm not a real Southerner, I would reply with a smirk.

When I think about being "Southern," I recall feelings of loss and pride, of hope and cynicism, of confidence and insecurity.

I look back to my own childhood: in my parent's backyard, always within spitting distance of a cow, and never too far away from a neighbor's Confederate flag. I knew I was Black, but was I really? We were the only Black family in our neighborhood for as long as I can remember, and the neighbors let us know it.

Until middle school, I did not attend school with more than a handful of other Black students. By then, the damage was done—as a child, surrounded by white children whose parents already thought they had my number, I decided early on that I would try to prove that I was not like "the others." I come from a stable home, I had parents who took care of me, I lived in a neighborhood with white folks, I would reassure them, convincing them (and perhaps myself), that I was worthy of consideration.

When I think about being Black and Southern, I look back at attending a majority-minority public school, one of the best public high schools in the state. Ironically, my parents put me in all-white schools because they knew what I did not yet understand about receiving a Southern-segregated education. What they could not have predicted is how their determination to make me well-adjusted and well-educated would have the unintended consequence of confusing the hell out of me. As a kid, I spent my formative years feeling like I had to explain myself away, because I thought it the most effective means of belonging, and lost part of my self-identification along the way.

I think about being one of the fewer than a handful of Black students in my gifted classes, and unironic conversations about the economic justifications of slavery. I think about finally coming into my Blackness, understanding that I come from a legacy of success through strife and being proud of that, and also contending with predominantly white spaces fighting back that pride at every turn.

I recall the days President Obama won: in 2008, watching my parents as they realized America's first Black president was just elected, and then going to school the next day to outcries from children whose parents told them that this country should keep the White House a *white* house; and in 2012, on the cusp of graduating high school and elated about reelection, and arriving at school the next day with friends warning me not to "be so loud" about my excitement.

I made a habit of reminding people of "the change we can believe in" after that.

When I think about being from the South, I think about Stacey Abrams.

And Coretta Scott King.

And Emma Gonzalez.

And Arekia Bennett.

And Mariah Parker.

I think about my siblings who raise my nieces and nephews in Louisiana, Texas, and Georgia. I think about my family's history in North Louisiana, which dates as far back as the late 1870s. I think about my mother and father, born and raised in Kentucky and Louisiana.

I think about the black and brown folks across the region, the majority of whom live in poverty—and how any propensity thriving in this region was built off the backs of our collective ancestors.

* * *

I decided to tell the stories of the young people in this region out of a desire to demonstrate that there are people who are unsupported in their steadfast goal to create progress.

In sharing these stories, I think about rebutting the everyday notion that investment in the South is futile, and about the people who look down from on high from the coasts and joke about secession or electoral failures. I think about what would have happened if people believed in Stacey Abrams's campaign for Georgia Governor early, or the countless other progressives whose campaigns fall into obsolescence because of a collective refusal to try.

I also think about myself several years ago. Throughout my childhood, I longed for the day that I could leave home, away from the identity crisis borne from being Black, but not Black *enough*, and feeling like I took up too much space that I was never supposed to occupy. From being lower income, splitting my time between families and compartmentalizing my family's struggles, finding refuge in books and the classroom but also in bad behavior and worse influences. From thinking differently than many of my peers, and wanting desperately to conform, because it would have been a lot easier than how I was feeling before.

I didn't realize that I would grow to feel deeply connected to that place. I worked hard in high school with the singular goal of getting the hell out of dodge. I took up to thirty hours a week at my part-time job to pay for my extracurricular activities and dual enrollment classes, hoping that my grades would get me on the first plane, train, or automobile out of Shreveport, Louisiana.

When I didn't get a scholarship to the out-of-state school that I wanted to attend, I decided to attend Louisiana State University instead (far enough, I thought), and leave as soon as I graduated college. I was laser-focused, and my goal was self-centered.

So when I entered my final year of college, with a literal one-way ticket out of Louisiana and into Mexico City to embark on a Fulbright scholarship, I didn't anticipate the sinking feeling I had in my stomach that I made the wrong decision to leave. Even though I continue to do work in the South, I have no idea when I will finally find my way back home full-time. At the end of the day, I believe I chose self-preservation over my passion for progress, at least temporarily.

I don't blame others who do the same. Particularly if you are marginalized, there is no real obligation to stay in a place that consistently denies your humanity. Every day in the South, marginalized people have to face the reality that many people with whom they share space would not care if marginalized people disappeared from the face of the Earth. The wounds of Jim Crow are not just fresh; they are open sores, getting more infected as time goes on and the sores remain untreated. I don't blame anyone who decided that it was not their job to close those wounds, who never felt the connection that I grew to feel, or who left and made a happier life for themselves in the comfort of a less outwardly marginalizing community. Like any choice regarding one's self care, there is no morally right or wrong answer, but rather a personal decision of priority.

But if you do choose to stay, understand that you are not choosing comfort. Instead, you are choosing difficult days, and you may regularly question your decision. You are also choosing a home that will hug your neck, a home with a history and a culture that is as rich as it is complicated, with its own dialect to boot.

You are not choosing to "save" the South; you are choosing to lift it up in spite of its past, and to progress it in spite of its present.

You are choosing to join like-minded young folks who are building the future they deserve and preserving the culture that they can be proud of.

You are choosing to be tried and tired every day, hoping one day to be desensitized to the constant state of crisis but never ceasing to be surprised at the inhumanity of it all.

You are choosing William Faulkner and Booker T. Washington and Martin Luther King.

You are choosing Southern hospitality and Southern contradictions.

You are choosing home.

* * *

Recently, I went to my favorite coffee shop in DC. I just got off the phone with my mother, my most consistent connection to home. I ordered an iced tea. It tasted bittersweet.

ACKNOWLEDGEMENTS

———

There would be nothing to acknowledge without the blood, sweat, and tears of the one who gave birth to me. To my mother, thank you for believing in all my goals, especially when the success of some are based entirely in your faith in me.

Thank you to New Degree Press, my publisher, for making this journey as easy as one could possibly make a process for a second-then-third year law student who decides to write a book. Thank you to Jordan Waterwash, Eric Koester, Brian Bies, Linda Berardelli, and the rest of the New Degrees Press crew for helping me bring my vision to fruition. To the *Bitter Southerner*, thank you for publishing the excerpt to "If Not Me, then Who?" and helping spread my message.

Writing something so personal has been tough for me, and I cannot imagine that it has been smooth on my friends, my family, or my partner. Thank you all for putting up with me — I know I don't always make it easy.

The source material are friends and friends of friends, and I cannot believe they took the time to support my work by spending so much time with me. To Dana Sweeney, Arekia Bennett, Raymond Partolan, Joey Wozniak, Megan Newsome, Helen Frink, Charlie Bonner, and Zöe Williamson — thank you for entrusting me with your stories, and I can only hope I did them justice.

I owe my career to The Andrew Goodman Foundation and to the Manship School of Communication at Louisiana State University. I owe my passion for writing to my teachers who brought me up at C.E. Byrd High School. I owe my passion for the South to the mentors from Shreveport to Baton Rouge who chose to take me under their wing. Thank y'all for teaching me.

This book was made better by the people who took the time to thoughtfully provide feedback. I am grateful and thankful to Nadia Hussein, Taryn Dwyer, Dana Sweeney, and Kristyn Turner for hitting me with the hard truths about my writing.

Last but certainly not least, I would like to thank everyone who first supported the development of my book by purchasing it early, effectively putting their faith in me to write something that they would want to read. These first contributors include Amanda Formica, Alicia Dixon, Alyssa Pooler, Andrea Fenster, Andrew Dam, Aneta Bhojwani Hopkins, Annie Flanagan, Benji Martinez, Brian Vanneman, Cary Joshi. Cedric Glover, Claire Hadlock, Clara Mora, Clarissa Unger, Cozette Jones, D'Angela Richardson, Dana Sweeney, Danielle Robinette, Dario Scalco, David Goodman, David Vines, Debra Hare, Devan Patel, Donovan Stone, Dorothy Joseph, Elizabeth Crivaro, Elizabeth Dellenger, Elizabeth Philipp, Ellen Watlington, Ellie Davis, Emily Turner, Eric Koester, Eric Kashdan, Evanne LeBlanc, Francesca Holt, Georgia Head, Gloria Richardson, Grace Ann Paras, Hunter Thompson, Jen Domagal-Goldman, Joey Wozniak, Janae Staicer, Janet Haynes, Jean McCurry, Jeevna Sheth, Jo Ripoll, Joanna Woodson, Jonian Rafti, Karen Zito, Karena Cronin, Kassidy Voinche, Kassie Phebillo, Katherine Rumer, Katrena Edwards, Kelsey Bordelon, Kristin Boggs, Kristyn Turner, Lauren Simenauer, Lisa Ann Markuson, Lorren Patterson, Lucas Almonte, MacKenzie Bills, Madison Dunman, Marisa Slifka, Mary Burleigh, Megan Newsome, Melissa Kestner-Clay, Micela Richardson, Michael Dyson, Michele Poole, Mikala Sanders, Nicole Carroll, Rachael Cohen Hamilton, Rachel Farkas, Rachel Finn, Rebecca Killian, Regina Parker, Robert Mann, Ronald Scott Novak

Jr, Sallie Gilbert, Sam Novey, Sophia Weinstock, Stephanie King, Thanh D Nguyen, Thomas Rodgers, Tina Tang, Ty Pinkins, Usjid Hameed, Virginia Bonner, Yark Beyan, and Zöe Williamson.

To all those who I missed, thank you. To all those who came before, thank you for leading and living by example.

www.ingramcontent.com/pod-product-compliance
Lightning Source LLC
Chambersburg PA
CBHW071524180526
45171CB00002B/370